small churches
are the
right size

small churches are the right size

DAVID R. RAY

The Pilgrim Press
New York

Library of Congress Cataloging in Publication Data

Ray, David R., 1942-
  Small churches are the right size.

  Includes bibliographical references.
  1. Small churches. I. Title.
BV637.8.R39 1982   254   82-11256
ISBN 0-8298-0620-2 (pbk.)

Scripture quotations, unless otherwise indicated, are from the
Revised Standard Version of the Bible, copyright 1946, 1952 and ·
© 1971 by the Division of Christian Education, National Council
of Churches, and are used by permission. Scripture quotations
marked TEV are from the *Good News Bible: Today's English
Version;* Old Testament: © American Bible Society, 1976; New
Testament: © American Bible Society 1966, 1971, 1976; used by
permission. Scripture quotations marked NEB are from *The New
English Bible,* © The Delegates of the Oxford University Press
and The Syndics of the Cambridge University Press 1961, 1970;
reprinted by permission. Scripture quotations marked JB are from
The Jerusalem Bible, copyright © 1966 by Darton, Longman &
Todd, Ltd. and Doubleday & Company, Inc.

The Pilgrim Press, 132 West 31 St., New York, NY 10001

CONTENTS

FOREWORD

In 1972, Hartford Seminary made a change in its programs giving major emphasis to education, consultation, and research services for churches and ministers. It was said at the time that a major test of the program would be its success in assisting parishes to be renewed. Much discussion ensued about the traits of a renewed parish. While there was never complete agreement, it was assumed that we would probably know one when we saw it.

The remarkable story told in the following pages supports that assumption. The Trinitarian Congregational Church of Warwick, Massachusetts and its pastor, David Ray, were involved in the seminary's program for several years. It seems clear that the congregation has undergone a significant experience of renewal—not simply because of its relationship to Hartford Seminary, but also through the efforts of its clergy and lay leaders, who were open to the renewing power of the Spirit of God.

The Warwick congregation's story is an especially important one because it is not only an example of a renewed parish, but a renewed small membership parish. While there is no intrinsic reason for surprise that a congregation with a small membership has experienced renewal, this is not the usual expectation, especially given cultural fascination with bigness. The recent emphasis on "small is beautiful" notwithstanding, American culture places great store on growth, and churches have not escaped this adulation of size. Church growth has become a high priority in most denominations, including mainline Protestantism. Some local congregations seem regularly to compete with one another for the largest membership or the biggest Sunday school. Clergy careers are typically judged to be successful by virtue of advancements from small to ever larger congregations. In all this, churches of small membership have at best been passed by in the fascination with growth and bigness, and at worst treated as second- or third-rate citizens. Not much is expected of them. They are not viewed as having great potential, and are often only "launching pads" for the careers of beginning pastors or "resting stations" for older clergy nearing retirement. These attitudes and low expectations persist in spite of the fact that between half and two thirds of all Protestant congregations have less than two hundred members, which is one definition of a small-membership church. Thus, to be able to point to a *very* small membership congregation, such as the one described in this book, as a model of a renewed parish is both unexpected and instructive. It is especially instructive because David Ray provides a helpful analysis of dimensions of the Warwick congregation's renewal and practical and useful suggestions. There are three aspects of the Warwick story that I would single out as especially important.

First, the analysis of possibilities for renewal in small churches is a wholistic one. Rather than singling out one aspect of a small church for attention—for example, its capacity for being a caring community—the author addresses the core tasks or functions of the church. I believe that every church, regardless of its size, must find ways of carrying out at least five core tasks. They include: (1) *worship*, by which a congregation affirms and honors its primary center of loyalty; (2) *education or socialization*, through which members learn the basic beliefs, values, history, and knowledge of the congregation's religious heritage; (3) *caring and building community*, through which members of the congregation experience a sense of belonging, conflict resolution, and commitment; (4) *mission or outreach*, by which the congregation seeks to influence its environment; and (5) *governance*, through which leaders and members establish goals and priorities, allocate roles and responsibilities, and develop the necessary resources to carry out their aims. The particular way a given congregation carries out these five core tasks will vary according to the congregation's size, resources, location, and other factors. The author provides helpful discussion of the ways that small congregations can be faithful and effective in carrying out their core tasks in relation to their size, resources, and situation. To be sure, the author provides no "quick fix" that can be readily applied to any small church. Careful analysis, imagination, creativity, and hard work are also required.

A second aspect of the Warwick story is the importance of creative clergy leadership. The pastor, although a key figure, is not the only actor in the drama. Could this church have undergone its transformation without David Ray? The answer is probably yes, but it would have taken someone very much like him in his stead. It would have required a person with imagination, creativity, and ability. Many clergy have these traits in varying measures, but they have to be willing to stay long enough in a particular parish to develop and use them. Commitment to a longer tenure in the small church than many ministers typically make is essential for renewal. I believe that much of David Ray's success is attributable to his relatively long ministry in the Warwick congregation.

A factor obviously working against long tenure is the low salary that most small churches can afford to pay a pastor. David Ray's experience demonstrates one way that this problem can be met creatively. He also demonstrates the other more psychic rewards, such as recognition and opportunity to exercise church leadership beyond the local congregation, which can be experienced without harming one's primary ministry within the congregation. Clergy considering the possibility of long-term commitments to small-church ministry, and lay leaders interested in attracting able clergy leadership, will find the author's example instructive.

Finally, the author demonstrates a third important lesson for small-church clergy and lay leaders. There are a number of outside resources available to small churches: denominational resources, seminary resources, and persons or groups with various consulting training skills. A small church should not be timid in making use of these resources. The

Warwick congregation demonstrates how investment in these resources enabled latent potential within the congregation to be developed and released.

No small membership church should attempt to duplicate Warwick's story. But laity and clergy alike can find in this book the inspiration to discover their congregation's potential, and a careful analysis of ways in which that potential can be released for renewal. To this end, I commend this book to you.

—JACKSON W. CARROLL

INTRODUCTION

Did you hear the one about the duck hunter who mail-ordered a fully trained retriever pup? After picking the dog up at the airport, the hunter stopped at a roadside pond to test the dog. He threw a stick across the pond and commanded, "Fetch!" The pup leaped for the water, *ran* across the water to the stick, picked it up, and *ran* back across the water. Astounded, the hunter repeatedly threw the stick, and the dog repeatedly retrieved it in the same unorthodox fashion.

Wanting to show off his remarkable dog, the hunter took his partner, George, out the next morning for a demonstration. With a knowing smile, the hunter threw a stick, gave the command, and the dog *ran* across the water and retrieved the stick. The hunter glanced proudly at George, who returned a noncommittal look. The stick was again thrown and retrieved, but still there was no response from George. Suppressing disappointment and irritation, the hunter demanded, "What do you think of my new dog?" After a long, disinterested pause, George answered, "Dog can't swim very well, can he?"

There is a strong resemblance between the unorthodox but gifted retriever and the very average yet remarkable small church in Warwick, Massachusetts, which I have pastored for the last eleven years. Compared to churches that carry the label "successful," this little church of fourteen active people in 1971 could not "swim" very well. At that time it was struggling to stay afloat. Today, while it may not swim like other churches, it certainly gets the job done.

The "problem" with most small churches is that they don't "swim" very well. They don't pay their ministers what the ministers need and usually deserve. Frequently their buildings are not adequate to house a full-service program. There is no program for every age and interest. They don't follow the recommended assessment and planning procedures. Denominations don't get the mission and program support money they expect. There may not be enough talented musicians for a good four-part harmony choir, not enough trained teachers and students for a modern church school program, not enough officers and committee members to satisfy the recommended model for a church organization, not enough worshipers to inspire great preaching efforts, and not enough givers to pay the oil bill. The small church may also not be big enough to gratify the ego needs of the pastor and the people.

The hunter's partner clearly had no use for a retriever that could not swim, even if the dog could run on water. Many church bureaucrats have been complaining for a long time about small churches that cannot swim. Loren B. Mead writes, "My experience with hundreds of those executives, bishops, and pastors makes me feel that no problem bears down upon them more heavily than 'the problem of the small congregation.'"[1]

Church researcher and consultant James L. Lowery Jr., cites a New York State Council of Churches statement from the 1960s that sets numerical minimum quotas for church viability: for fellowship and worship, 50 persons; for property ownership, 200 members; and for a total pastoral unit (the number served by one professional pastor), 350 members (400 where two buildings must be kept up). "Below these is a small non-viable church or congregation."[2] Lowery then makes his own conclusion:

> The existence of a surprisingly large number of non-viable, small churches is a large fact of life in many denominations. And they can't be closed down! They survive, hang on by the fingernails, and do little else. . . . [The small church] is a problem because it is not viable. It is too small, too poor, and too focused on its own institutional survival to be able to carry on

meaningful worship, in depth pastoral ministry, and effective witness, service, and missionary work. In a phrase, it is *unable to be very Christian.*

But the paradoxical thing about the same situation is that those small churches very often draw a constituency who *like a size too small* to be viable while they do not like its lack of ministry. And this constituency is on the whole *very loyal, very strong in attendance,* and *more avid in the sharing of time, talent, and focus.*"[3]

The writer seems distressed by the plight of the poor, nonviable, nonswimming small churches. He seems not to recognize how significant it is that the same "not-viable . . . too small, too poor . . . unable to be very Christian churches" have the running-on-water attributes of being "very loyal, very strong in attendance, and more avid in the sharing of time, talent, and focus." He seems not to understand that though small and poor, they can be very Christian and can carry on meaningful worship, real pastoral ministry, and effective witness, service, and missionary work.

If a small church cannot be closed, it must be capable of living, and the jury is still out on whether most of these "nonviable" churches have the ability to grow, expand, and develop. Eleven years ago many experts would have wanted to close the church I serve, yet it is both alive and growing.

For a long time much effort was devoted to trying to encourage, teach, and require these small, nonswimming churches to swim. They were expected to measure up to the prescribed salary standard, to use the prescribed curriculum, to participate in all the special offerings, to raise the expected judicatory support money, to have the prescribed organizational structure, to have graded church school classes, and so on. When they failed their swimming test, they were pronounced nonviable.

Carl Dudley concludes, "[The small congregation] does not fit the organizational model for management efficiency. It does not conform to the program expectations of 'something for everyone.' It does not provide expanding resources for professional compensation. It is not a 'success.'"[4] One frustrated denominational leader complained, "The small church is the toughest, because it won't grow and it won't go away."[5] What few have appreciated or understood is that most of these small churches were at least staying afloat, and many were indeed running on water like that retriever.

Currently there is an effort in church and society to purge individuals and institutions of racism and sexism. Generally the church has recognized that by responding to minorities and women in a prejudicial and discriminatory way, it is dealing unjustly and being deprived of a rich reservoir of energy and expertise. There is another "ism" that should be purged from the collective consciousness of church and society: the "ism" of "sizism." Permeating our consciousness is an assumption that smaller is lesser and bigger is better. In the world of the church, it is the churches with the biggest Sunday school, the biggest mission budget, the biggest membership, the biggest fleet of buses, or the biggest building that get the biggest press and prizes.

Size is a convenient yardstick for measuring stature and performance, but it can confuse quantity with quality, popularity with authenticity. God calls the church not to be big but to be faithful and effective. There is no inherent virtue in bigness, and neither is there sin in smallness. The Christian church is pervaded with sizism, to the detriment of all churches, big and small. Without sizism, we could ask not how big is your building, budget, Sunday school, or membership, but how faithful and effective is your ministry and mission?

This book will be useful for several audiences. Both clergy and laity will benefit from a consideration of the themes, issues, and ideas presented here and can use them to stimulate and guide their shared ministry and life. College and seminary students who are considering parish ministry as their vocation will also find the book thought-provoking and practical. And for seminary and denominational people there are fresh and real implications for their work with both the small and larger organs of the Body of Christ, the Christian church.

My purpose is, first, to demonstrate that *small churches are the right size*—the right size for being faithful and effective churches. The New Testament image of what a church is and should be is close to that which can happen naturally in small churches. Throughout most of church history almost all churches were small, yet the thesis that small churches are the right size to be fully the church is a radical one. Carl Dudley, one of the most sympathetic advocates of small churches, suggests that "the small congregation is the appropriate size for only one purpose: the members can know one another personally."[6] But that is not true, for fewer people can also contribute to a more intimate and highly participatory worship, individualized and experiential education, the mobilization of the whole congregation in mission, a family-style caring network, an organizational model that is simple and economical to maintain, and a ministry in which all parts of the body have a place and purpose.

Like any church, small churches have their problems. They can be ingrown, fractious, and provincial; they can use their small size as an excuse for inactivity and mediocrity. Many of their problems stem from attempting to be something they are not—big. Buildings, budgets, programs, and expectations that were too big have squashed many small churches.

Just as there are advantages to smallness, there are advantages to largeness. God needs all sizes in the struggle to redeem this prodigal society. I am focusing on small churches because they are frequently overlooked and misunderstood in the ecclesiastical world and because I have discovered that in the small church family people can be especially Christian, productive, and at home.

My second purpose is to demonstrate that small churches think, feel, and act differently from large churches. A Great Dane is a different breed from a dachshund; the two breeds look different, act differently, serve different purposes, and have different appeal. The same is true of churches, but frequently this is either minimized or never recognized as churches plan. The result is confusion and failure. I will suggest how a small church can worship, educate, care, serve, and maintain itself in ways uniquely appropriate to its size.

As a small-church pastor, I am familiar with the realities,

problems, and possibilities of small churches. I have been the part-time pastor of a 150-year-old, typical New England church for eleven years. The rest of my time has been invested as a student, househusband, crisis center director, pastoral counselor, community organizer, teacher, and church consultant. My parishioners have taught me, I have taught them, and we've learned well together. Before and during my doctoral work at Hartford Seminary, I read and studied all I could find about small churches. As a member of the Massachusetts Conference (United Church of Christ) Small Church Task Force, I designed and administered a revealing survey of our conference's small churches. I have conducted a variety of small-church workshops. As a part-time UCC Conference Christian Education Consultant and a member of Hartford Seminary's adjunct faculty, I have had opportunities to work in a variety of churches. From all these associations with small-church people, I have developed a theoretical understanding of small churches and gleaned a multitude of ideas and tools.

The Warwick church is an "average" small church in that its people are hardworking, unsophisticated, economically lower and middle income, not highly educated, and not especially practiced in the art of church management. It is remarkable in that the people are dedicated, responsive, and faithful. The church is usually harmonious, lively, growing, and now believes "we can do anything we want to do." The church is the way it is because of God's grace, committed people, sound principles, wise decisions, and hard work. Our worship is intimate and enriching, our education is experiential and effective, our people care for one another, our mission is targeted at specific needs in the local community and the larger world, and we can pay our bills and solve our problems.

Our membership has grown from thirty to seventy during the time Warwick's population increased by 25 percent. Our worship attendance has grown from a dozen or so to about sixty-five. Our budget has expanded from $1,500 to $19,000. Our building is a restored and expanded 1816 colonial house. Our people have gone to seminary with their pastor.

Yet by some standards, this is a nonviable church—one that cannot swim. But it can run on water.

There are many other small churches as vital and viable as this one, and many if not most others can be. It is hoped that struggling churches will find here inspiration and practical ideas that will help them swim, run, dive, fly, or whatever is natural to them and responsive to God's calling.

The roots of the current interest in small churches go back over half a century. Between 1900 and 1920 several fascinating books chronicled the Rural Church Movement, preaching the need for a resurgence in the rural church so that it could lead a resurgence in rural life. This movement went the way of most other movements, yet the need still exists. The 1970s saw a new movement—the Small Church Movement, in which the focus is no longer just rural. It has been recognized that small churches are found in every setting and that their particularity must be addressed. There are small-church newsletters, small-church conferences, small-church issues of ecclesiastical magazines, small-church books, and small-church lobbyists raising the voice of the small church in a variety of forums. This renewed interest in small churches was a recognition of the needs of small churches and the need for them.

Why another resource on small churches?

- None of the better resources are based on firsthand experience with small churches.
- Most have focused on the *problems* of small churches, rather than their possibilities.
- While some have recognized the distinctiveness of small churches, they have not developed the theological and biblical imagery and insights that provide a solid direction and foundation for a renewed small church.
- They have not dealt seriously or specifically with the unique nature and opportunities inherent in the basic tasks of the church as they are carried out in small churches—worship, education, mission, caring, and maintenance.
- They have not provided small-church leaders with

enough tools and ideas for assessing, planning, and programming.

The following chapters proceed from illustration to definition to application. The first chapter is the story of the Warwick church's decade of transformation. It is offered not as a model of how to do it, but as an illustration of how one small church was revitalized. It illustrates the principles and practices described in later chapters. The reader might prefer to read it as the last chapter.

The central premise of Chapter 2 is that the size of an organization is a critical factor in how it functions and that therefore a small church needs to think and work in ways appropriate to its size. The chapter summarizes how others have understood "small church" and then suggests that a small church is not a limited version of the real thing but rather any church that embodies certain size-influenced qualities that can help it function in unique and very Christian ways. These qualities are found most often in churches with a small number of participants.

Chapters 3 to 7 are devoted to what I see as the five basic tasks of the church: worship, education, mission, caring, and maintenance. Others have come up with different lists of tasks. A church that ignores or merely gives lip service to any of these tasks will soon falter and eventually fail as a Christian church, for it will not be faithful to its calling or effective in its work. All churches are called to the same tasks, but all churches will not do them in the same way. A wise small church will do each of these tasks in a unique and distinctive way. Regardless of how few the people, small churches are the right size and fully equipped to do these basic tasks. If they fail, it is not because of limited numbers but because of limited vision, limited resourcefulness, or limited commitment—or because they are trying to act like a church of a different size. These chapters will discuss how small churches can most authentically and successfully worship, learn, serve, care, and maintain themselves.

Chapter 8 addresses ministry in small churches. Ministry is understood as a calling of all the people of God, not as merely a professional role. Lay and clergy ministry will look and work differently in small churches. This chapter high-lights bi-vocational ministry as one effective and affordable form of trained pastoral leadership.

I hope the reader will find here a balanced, nutritious meal of theory, application, and illustration which will spice, nourish, and flesh out the reader's involvement in and with small churches. May your reading be tasty, digestible, and energizing.

small churches
are the
right size

CHAPTER 1

a dream come true

For consider your call . . . not many of you were wise according to worldly standards, not many were powerful, not many were of noble birth; but God chose what is foolish in the world to shame the wise, God chose what is weak in the world to shame the strong, God chose what is low and despised in the world, even things that are not, to bring to nothing things that are, so that no human being might boast in the presence of God. He is the source of your life in Christ Jesus.
—1 Corinthians 1:26-30

This chapter tells the story of the renewal of the Trinitarian Congregational Church of Warwick, Massachusetts. It is told not to boast, but simply to illustrate what is possible for virtually any small, struggling church. Eleven years ago many would have despaired over this church. Churches like it had been closed all over America. By accepted standards of success, this church would have been considered "foolish," "weak," "low," and "despised."

What happened to this church in the 1970s has been dramatic and is a drama that is still playing. The original cast from 1971 included fourteen active members, five men and nine women, and the new minister and his wife. Six of the fourteen were past retirement age. One or two had some college education. These were typical people found in a rural, factory-worker community. There were no active young people, except for the handful of Sunday school children. It was the first parish for the new part-time minister.

This was an unlikely cast to be the nucleus of a renewed church. Most tiny churches would have as much innate ability and potential. What the church had going for it was a committed and responsive core membership, an energetic pastor with ideas, people in the community waiting for a lively church, and a gracious God.

The setting for this drama was also unlikely. The Metcalf Memorial Chapel was and is the home of the Trinitarian Congregational Church. The building is an 1816 colonial house. The original Congregational church building was sold and razed at the time of the first federation with the Unitarian church in 1929. After the federation was broken, the church members worshiped in homes and in a barn until the house was purchased and turned into a chapel in 1937. It was named after the Rev. Harlan Metcalf, a retired minister, who had led the church during those difficult transition years.

In 1971 the building had two rooms that were heated, an attached outhouse, no running water, questionable wiring, and decaying foundation sills and floor beams. One room was used for worship and one for Sunday school. At the time the new minister arrived, an average Sunday would find up to a dozen children and two teachers in Sunday school, up to a dozen adults with a two-person choir as the congregation, and a visiting lay or retired preacher filling the pulpit.

This was the only active church in a community of 492 people. The Unitarian church was largely inactive, and some residents attended churches in surrounding towns. Warwick is a beautiful heavily wooded hill-town nestled at the foot of Mount Grace in western Massachusetts. The town and area was economically depressed. The population was a combination of retired people; factory, foundry, and paper mill workers and their families; young adults who moved here as part of the return to agrarian values and ways; a few self-employed loggers, carpenters, and farmers; and a handful of merchants and professionals. The only businesses were the general store, the Warwick Inn, and a sawmill. In the last decade the town has grown to about 550 people. It is

4

still the same kind of community with the same kind of people.

An interesting and difficult dynamic is that Warwick is about twenty miles from four large communities in four different directions and three different states. Therefore Warwick travels in four directions to work, shop, play, and receive services. Elementary school children attend a local three-room school, and junior high and high school students are bused to a regional school. There is no single newspaper or radio station that serves the town. People cannot even get the same television channels because of the signal-blocking presence of Mount Grace. As a result, more divides the community than draws it together. Again, one would not expect this typical sleepy New England town to be the setting for a resurgent church.

The church had two federations with the Unitarians, neither of which lasted. There had been no resident Congregational minister in decades. Its listed membership was about the same as it was at its founding 142 years earlier —thirty. This church was similar to the other thousands of tiny churches that dot America's urban and rural landscape —struggling to pay bills, attract leadership, recruit members, meet needs, and remain alive. Charles Morse, our church and town historian, wrote the story of our church in 1969. He described it as

> a typical small rural church which has had a continuous struggle to exist from the day of its birth. It still struggles and it still exists. . . . We are proud of the difficulties we have overcome, and we hope our story will be an inspiration to our fellow churches.[1]

Our church today, though still quite small, is vastly different from what it was then. Yet we would not be who we are if it had not been for those few who fought the good fight and kept the faith.

PROLOGUE

The prologue to our drama is the dream of one of our actors. Rotha Nordstedt is a very special and important person. Hard of hearing and hardworking, she is one of our unlikely heroines. This is her account of a recurring dream she had prior to my arrival.

> With all the struggles that we went through, we would get so discouraged and I would say to Carl: "Let's keep going, let's hang on, something is bound to come out of this. We just can't fold up. Wouldn't it be ideal if we would get a fine young minister?" We just kept hoping and hanging on with the hope that some day somebody would have an interest. . . . I remember waking more than once thinking what will become of our little church? . . . My biggest dream was to have someone come and rescue us.

Like many dramas, ours has been a drama in three acts. There have been three distinct phases in our life together. As with a drama, Act I was the time of identifying the actors, beginning the action, and developing the themes. Act II was a time of great action and movement. Act III has been a time of internal growth, redefinition, and recovenanting.

ACT I

After seminary in 1968, I accepted a position as director of the new Brattleboro (Vermont) Area Youth Ministry. My wife accepted a teaching position at the Brattleboro high school. When we discovered that New England was to be home for us we began looking for a piece of land that could be "ours." An affordable twenty-acre woodlot was found twenty miles away in Warwick. While building a log chalet on our "Grace Farm," we noticed the sign on a colonial house in town identifying it as a Congregational chapel. On a Sunday free of Brattleboro responsibilities, we attended a service at the chapel. The atmosphere was quaint, warm, and friendly. On the way home I fantasized out loud about being the pastor of that little church.

By winter of 1970 it was clear that an ecumenical youth ministry was no longer a priority for the sponsoring Brattleboro churches. I wondered if teaching might be a better profession for me than ministry and started a master's degree program in education. The crisis center I helped start offered to employ me two days a week. But I was not ready to give up on the church.

Our nearest Warwick neighbor referred me to Mr. Morse, moderator and one of the pillars at the chapel. I carefully inquired if the church might be interested in a part-time resident minister. He thought they might and offered to check with the others. In the spring I was added to the rotation of visiting worship leaders, and in the summer I was the regular leader of worship. On August 8, 1971, I was called as their two-day-a-week pastor for sixty dollars a week. In Charles Morse's 1979 epilogue to his 1969 booklet, he wrote: "This appeared to be the answer to our prayer for a resident settled minister who could perform pastoral duties and instill new life in our church."[2]

In the sermon I preached on August 8, I placed a challenge and a dream before the church members as they prepared to call their first "settled" pastor in many years:

> Today is a day of decision for you. Some of you are concerned with what the decision means for you financially. And as good "Yankees" that is understandable. But effort to meet a greater financial obligation is only a surface issue in the decision you have to make. The real decision is whether you are content with the way things are now.

> • Are you content with a church that for the most part is in existence one hour a week?
> • Are you content with the divisions, conflicts, and misunderstandings in this community?
> • Are you content that nothing more needs to be offered for the children, youth, and adults of Warwick?
> • Are you content that the lonely, the sick, the upset don't really need more attention?
> • Are you content in the belief that Warwick doesn't need a more active church?
> The decision you have to make is composed of those questions and others. The decision is whether you are content or whether you see a need, a challenge, a job that needs to be done. . . .
> You should be warned that all of these challenges, these needs, don't get met in the working hours of someone employed two days a week. These things get done

when there are new ideas, leadership, and people who are so concerned they are willing to join together and go to work. . . .

I have a dream for this church and for Warwick. My dream is that this church will choose to embark on a new adventure. My dream is that we could rediscover that energy, ability, financial, and personal resources put to work would return to us and to the town far more than we originally expended. My dream is that Warwick will become a healthier place to live, a place that understands its problems and knows how to solve them. That's my dream. What's yours?

Although I had never heard the words, I was now a bi-vocational or tentmaker minister. I had happened into a style of life and ministry that many others are choosing by necessity or by choice. It is a form of ministry that has a noteworthy beginning. The apostle Paul went to Corinth and stayed with Aquila and his wife, Priscilla, while he recruited for a new church in that community. "He went to see them; and because he was of the same trade he stayed with them, and they worked, for by trade they were tentmakers [Acts 18:2-3]." This is one very viable solution to the leadership and financial problems faced by many small churches, and for me it has been a satisfying and creative way to live and minister.

It was no small matter for the church to call me at $60 a week. Their total 1971 budget was $1,585. By calling me they were more than doubling their budget to $3,665. Instead of needing $30 a week to meet expenses, they would now need $70. This was a large and faithful step for fourteen active members, half of whom were on retirement incomes, the other half living on low to moderate incomes.

This was a first step toward effective action. They decided to be more vigorous in encouraging the use of offering envelopes. Three men built a "paper shack" at the town dump with salvaged materials for a paper recycling program that would raise some money. One Sunday the Nordstedts drove eighty miles and paid a surprise call on the UCC area minister to ask him for conference help; a $500 grant was forthcoming. The women's Christian Service

Society was revived. They donated a sum of money from their treasury and worked with new vigor on their traditional fair.

Inactives and community people were invited to church to meet "our new minister." For the first time in years there was a local pastor visiting in the community and calling on sick people. A senior high youth group was started. Interest was revived, attendance increased, and there was more than enough income to pay the bills. These were first steps in developing a "can do" attitude.

We've shared memories and checked records in an effort to ferret out the keys to the metamorphosis of this church. From our collective recollection and my interpretation, I can identify several attributes that were present before I arrived.

- There was a shared sense of pride and satisfaction that the church had survived.
- Several times neighboring churches and state denominational officials had helped them feel not alone and abandoned.
- The little remnant was loyal and hardworking. The church's survival was clearly a priority to them.
- The church had always managed to live within its means, so there was no feeling of financial futility or panic.
- There was a genuine feeling of mutual respect and appreciation. Mr. Morse wrote prior to my coming: "There are so many who have worked and sacrificed much because of their love and their belief in its worth, and whose names cannot be mentioned. Where would we begin, and where would we end?"[3]
- The church wanted to live, and therefore it was open to new ideas and new people. Both new ways and new people were received with interest and appreciation.

The presence of these qualities was a solid foundation on which to build. Despite a minimum of people, a shortage of resources, a lack of theological and biblical awareness, and inexperienced leadership, we still had a wealth of positive

9

qualities to undergird our pilgrimage. There was also some hesitance and Yankee conservatism as we began moving. However, the prevailing feeling was "Let's try."

As the protagonist in this drama, I utilized several approaches in initiating, facilitating, and supporting our transformation. While some were intentional, most were intuitive and, I hope, Spirit-led. The principles behind these approaches would be my ten commandments for any small-church leadership and renewal.

1. *Innovation.* We began with innovations. The traditional advice is to start slowly, but for the first service after I was called, I borrowed the elementary school's ditto machine and printed an order of worship, which the church had never had. I began to change the order of worship to make it more contemporary, flexible, personal, and appropriate for the setting. Within two weeks we instituted a coffee hour after worship—now an institution. Communion was changed from a quarterly observance to a monthly one. Why did we move so quickly? Interest was high. New people were trying us out. It was a new day. By calling me, the church members had already committed themselves to new possibilities. It was important to demonstrate that there were different ways, which could make our life together richer, more alive, and more rewarding. Innovations were introduced with an explanation and with the assurance that each was a trial and could be discontinued. Key people were consulted first, members were asked to help with the changes, and reservations and criticisms were listened to. And when something was different, something else was always the same. One veteran expressed it this way, "I like it because something is always different. We don't go to sleep anymore."

2. *Action.* Related to innovation, we began with lots of activity. There was the newspaper recycling project. Women were enlisted to bake bread for communion. The Christian Service Society was revived. A Stanley party was held to get a coffee maker for the coffee hour. The Sunday school collected for UNICEF and sold light bulbs to raise money for materials. The new youth group renovated a room for

themselves. We wanted to capitalize on the new and fresh interest and energy. We wanted to communicate quickly and clearly to the community that things were happening at the chapel. We wanted our people to experience immediately the excitement of what was possible for them, of what it would be like to have a church that was more than an hour of Sunday school and worship. We wanted people to enjoy themselves and one another.

3. *Success.* We sought to build success upon success. In the beginning I tried to lead them in ventures that had a high probability of success. I knew a coffee hour would be feasible and well received. I knew there were young people and parents hungry for local youth activity, so the youth group was started. I was confident that a Christmas Eve candlelight service would kindle community support, so this tradition was successfully begun. By building success upon success, the feeling began to catch hold that though the church was small, it could accomplish what it set out to do. The small-church syndrome of inferiority and futility was transformed into a feeling of confidence and adventure. This was my strategy for helping the church trust my leadership. The result was that eleven months later the church risked holding an auction, a food sale, and a public supper, which netted $1,800 in one day—an unprecedented accomplishment for them.

4. *Children and youth.* We brought children and youth into our midst. The youth group and a monthly family worship service were initiated, and the language and style of worship were made more comprehensible to younger people. Our church should be a place where families would come together and be together, for the nature of children and youth is to radiate vitality and hope. One of our grandmothers has affirmed, "One nice thing about the church is all the kids running around." One result has been that two of those young people attracted eleven years ago are now pillars in our church. Many people choose to raise families in small towns, and many of these will search out a church that supports and enables family life.

5. *Community outreach*. We reached out to the community from the beginning. Within two weeks I had mailed a letter to the people of the community introducing myself and what we were doing as a church. The letter invited their participation and offered a pastoral call. People invited other people. Children from the church went door-to-door collecting for UNICEF and selling light bulbs. Visitors were identified and made to feel welcome and needed. Time was taken in worship to share news about who was sick or hospitalized, who had moved to town, birthdays and anniversaries, and community events. I worked at developing the concept that the town was our parish (we had thirty-plus members, but a parish of 492). I made an effort to visit all from the community who were hospitalized, and not just those from the church. A chain reaction began. There was a new minister, new activity, new energy and ideas, and as the church demonstrated it cared, other people came. When new people joined us they were invited to assume responsibility in the church. We created new committees, enlarged old ones, and started new projects. As this all happened the original cast was pleased to see the interest, rewarded for the initial risk they had taken, and appreciated by the newer people for their faithfulness over the years. As a result of the effort to reach out, people became aware that this was not a closed little club but a church that was part of its community.

6. *Commendation and recognition*. From the beginning I was careful to appreciate, applaud, and affirm. In my first sermon I commended the congregation even as I challenged them: "You have done much in keeping this church alive. Hundreds and hundreds of hours of dedicated work have gone into this church. . . . And yet the needs of Warwick, in fact your own needs, probably say that the preservation of the Metcalf Chapel is not enough." "Thank you" is a staple in my vocabulary. If someone says something complimentary to me about someone else, I ask and suggest, "Have you told them that?" People working hard to keep struggling churches afloat are prone to ask themselves, "Why am I doing this?" or "What does it matter?" People who work hard

for their church often feel that it is a thankless activity. The only way we were going to keep our church motivated and moving was for the workers to feel needed and appreciated. One of the first meals we shared as a church was in the second fall when the newcomers put on an "appreciation luncheon" after worship for the veterans of the church. This followed a time of recognition during worship.

7. *Vision.* I am a goal-oriented person and tried to keep a vision before the church and encourage their own envisioning. Carl Sandburg wrote, "Nothing happens unless first a dream."[4] Each Sunday in my first month I preached about my vision or dream for the church in its worship, Christian education, and responsibility to the community. I used the development of the church in the unlikely city of Antioch (Acts 11:19-26) to summarize my dream for the unlikely church in Warwick:

> God has always used unlikely places for the setting of great things. . . . I really believe that in the tiny town of Warwick . . . God can accomplish something really significant through this church. . . . I think we can show how a rural church can be in step with the times; vital to the preservation, life, and development of its community; and dedicated to its faith.

We have kept a goal before us. My ministry has been focused on providing leadership for a pilgrim people. There have been such challenges as a larger budget, a significant mission project, a community project, a growth goal, a building improvement or addition, and our association with Hartford Seminary. Always the goal was realistic enough to be achievable—if we stretched and trusted. It is easy in a small, rural community to let the world go by. It would be easy for this church to sit back in self-satisfaction. However, the momentum will continue, the morale will remain high, and our discipleship will be faithful, *only* if we continue pursuing a vision.

8. *World-consciousness.* From the beginning we worked on a consciousness of the larger church and larger world. There was the UNICEF collection. We borrowed a projector and

showed a film about the mission program of the United Church of Christ. That first year and for the first time, we participated in the One Great Hour of Sharing Offering. Our treasurer had been refusing to send our small mission pledge to the denomination because of a disagreement about some of its use. Other church officers and I insisted the money be sent. Each year we increased our budget designation for mission. The youth group collected for the Heart Fund and put on a breakfast for Heifer Project International. By connecting our church and ourselves with something larger, we could transcend our feelings of insignificance. If we could relate in a meaningful way to issues, needs, and programs beyond our town lines, we could shake some of our small-town provincialism.

9. *Worship, the center.* Worship remained at the center of our life. It had been the only time the church members gathered. Unless our worship was alive and spirit-filled, nothing else would be. I worked to make our worship more personal and real. The order of worship was changed. Worshipers were helped to become participants rather than spectators. Even though some of the innovations were met with reservations, people agreed that everything did not have to please everyone. We added new hymns and songs and soon had a supplemental songbook. The choir grew, stopped wearing their robes, and became part of the congregation. They bought inexpensive recorders, learned to play them, and occasionally used them in worship.

The church year was celebrated. A birthday party for Jesus, with cake, was one Advent worship event. The youth group rounded up animals and costumes and had a live manger scene before our new Christmas Eve candlelight service. There was a Good Friday service and an Easter sunrise service and breakfast. All these worship experiences were new to the church and the community. A spring outdoor worship and church picnic—usually on Pentecost —became an annual tradition.

10. *A commitment to the people.* A final difficult but important principle was my commitment to the people.

Several voiced the conviction that I would stay a year or two and move to something bigger and better. "Why would he stay in this little church on what we pay him?" Repeatedly we made it clear that Warwick was our home, that between my wife's income and mine we could afford to stay. On several occasions I said I planned to stay as long as the church was responsive. My commitment was perceived in the financial sacrifice I was making, the time and energy I put into my ministry with them, and the real love I had for the people of our church. As people began to believe my commitment to them, they became more willing to dream bigger dreams and to make bigger commitments. A church will not follow leadership they cannot trust.

The years 1972, 1973, and 1974 continued the directions and initiatives of our first year. The church grew steadily. Several Catholics and various types of Protestants made us a truly ecumenical and community church.

Fall 1972 was significant for the church for another reason. Miss Alice Anderson, who had been semi-active in the church, suffered a stroke in February 1972 and died in September. In appreciation for our care during her illness, Alice had included the church in her will. To the shock of all, that bequest turned out to be almost $70,000. The two years it took to probate her will gave us time to plan its best use.

By 1974 the church was thinking beyond survival. Instead of two dozen people using our building once a week, about seventy were using the building several times a week. There were about thirty-five in worship and another thirty-five in the weekday church school. The budget had increased from $1,585 to $6,433 in three years. Instead of twelve families pledging, there were twenty. Almost all the members had at least doubled their giving. A variety of mission efforts were being supported. Morale, trust, and confidence were high. We were ready to face new challenges and to capitalize on new opportunities.

ACT II

The year 1975 was critical in the life of the Warwick church. It was a year in which we responded to two large challenges.

Steve Fellows, a local farmer's son, was a shy first-year college student in 1971. He joined our new youth group, choir, and the church and was added to our trustees. After a year in the Peace Corps, Steve indicated that he wanted to spend a year volunteering with Heifer Project International (an international agricultural assistance and development program), and he wanted to find a sponsor to cover the $1,800 stipend Heifer Project pays its volunteers.

Steve came to the Church Committee (our official board) and described the program and his intentions. Responses ranged from pessimism to optimism to the decision to try raising the $1,800. No one said "no" or "impossible." Accepting this challenge meant that we would be trying to raise $9,191 in 1975, in contrast to our 1974 budget of $6,433. It also meant we would be raising money for Heifer Project at the same time we were building an addition to our old building with volunteer labor.

In one January 1975 worship service we circulated a check received from the Anderson bequest, received ten new members, and kicked off our Heifer Project initiative. We commissioned Steve as our ambassador. Using Jesus' parable of the talents as an example, one, five, or ten dollar bills were given to those who would accept the challenge of "investing" the money to raise more money toward our Heifer Project goal.

Steve drove to Arkansas to the Heifer Project ranch, and the church buckled down to meet its challenge. There was a January supper. Cindy and I went to Guatemala on a Heifer Project work-study trip and came back with a personal report of Heifer Project's work and $100 worth of Guatemalan jewelry, clothing, and crafts. The sale of those items earned $200. Heifer Project T-shirts and greeting cards were sold. Donations came from the community. We brought a circus to town. A double walkathon was planned; about fifty walkers walked ten miles from each of two neighboring towns, met at the Warwick town common, and produced $1,350 in pledges.

For the church the talent investment project was the most significant. One person bought peas and planted, harvested, and sold them. Another bought ingredients and made and sold bread. I bought ten sap buckets and made and sold maple syrup. A new member bought gas and oil for his chain saw, cut a cord of firewood, and sold it. A calf was sold. Crafts were made and sold. Gradually the "talents" came in. The sum of $150 was turned into almost $800. Other projects were undertaken. By January 1976, some $2,700 had been earned, and within a few months the total was over $3,000—almost twice our goal.

As we reminisced about our Heifer Project involvement, a lay person confessed, "There were a lot of things about it, such as the innovative ideas about making money, that were frightening to me. But I think we all grew." And we did. We discovered that we could not predict our limits. Another success was notched, morale was higher, and visions were expanded. Today two framed certificates, a huge banner, and an inlaid wood-framed logo from Heifer Project serve as reminders of this remarkable experience.

The second 1975 challenge was the restoration of our chapel and an addition to it. What turned out to be a major undertaking began with small steps.

As we began to get some idea of the size of the Alice Anderson bequest, people began to talk about how the money should be used. By this time (1973) we were filling our small worship room, were in need of more Christian education space, and were worried about our ancient wiring and wishing for running water and toilets. Some people began to talk of building a "real" church building to replace the house we were using. A couple of mothers hoped for a church big enough for their daughters' weddings. Others talked of various remodeling and renovation schemes.

We were faced with three key questions:

- What is the prudent and appropriate thing to do with the Anderson money?
- What are and will be our building needs?
- How do we best go about meeting these needs?

I had other concerns related to these questions: that we not allow the Anderson money to become a crutch which would lead us to abdicate on our own responsibilities; that we not build a "real" church just to have one as nice as the empty

Unitarian church on the hill; that whatever we built should be functional, energy efficient, attractive, and large enough to allow for future growth; that the building should serve the church and the community rather than being a jewel we have to protect or a burden we have to support; that whatever we did should be done with consensus of all, rather than merely that of a select or expert committee.

From mid-1973 until groundbreaking, June 1, 1975, these questions and concerns were part of sermons, committee meetings, informal conversations, and whole church meetings. Ideas were encouraged and needs were assessed. Different options considered were: a new, traditional New England steepled church; a log church; a renovated chapel; an expansion; a whole new addition.

As we worked toward a decision, we encountered some prophetic words:

> How does the church speak to its community through its building? Modern architects have tended to express the church's uniqueness by making its place of worship different from the buildings which surround it. . . . Is not the best road for church architecture a far more modest one: namely, to return to the traditional practice of building in very ordinary external forms, utilizing function as the primary criterion? This may mean going back quite literally to the "house church" of a far earlier period.
>
> Internally such a return to simplicity would express the idea of the church building as a gathering place for the Christian family; externally it would mean that the church would look very much like the homes in its neighborhood. . . .
>
> Nothing is closer to the meaning of the church as a congregation than a home. Such qualities as hospitality, friendliness, communal life, all these, find their expression best in a simple human house.[5]

In an April 1974 sermon, I used that quotation to express the developing consensus and suggested that the Metcalf Chapel "is theologically correct—it says who we are and what we believe." We decided to keep the chapel as our home. We wanted to restore its appearance to symbolize the importance we place on our faith and God's work; to build a larger, more aesthetically pleasing worship room; to make our building more versatile, usable, and accessible by all ages, so that it could better serve our community; to make it an energy-efficient and economical example of good stewardship.

We then had to decide how much to do. As a church we talked and talked. Our trustees were charged with developing a proposal. Gradually a plan evolved. A church meeting was called for the evening of April 27, 1975. We unanimously voted to renovate and restore the chapel to near its original form; to raze the back wing, outhouse, and shed; and to build a new, larger worship room over a new dining room and kitchen. The building project would include a well, plumbing, new wiring, full insulation, and central heat. This would be financed with $30,000, or almost half the Anderson money. It would be accomplished with volunteer labor, except for one paid carpenter-foreman and the excavation, electrical, and plumbing work.

On June 1, 1975 we broke ground as part of our communion worship. In the sermon I suggested, "With the new opportunities of good space, come new responsibilities," and asked:

Are we building this as our house, for our egos and glory, for our comfort, and our use? Or are we building this as God's house, for worship and for service to any and all of God's children? Will we retreat here for peace and quiet and security? Or will we come here for insight, strength, courage, and cooperative work?

After the pastoral prayer we went out in a drizzle to break ground and bread. It was a memorable beginning.

About fifty volunteers participated, although about a dozen did the bulk of the labor. Two of our members worked almost full-time as volunteer helpers of our paid carpenter. The process was as significant as the product. There were days when work went undone because there weren't enough volunteers. For example, one summer Saturday the framed walls could not be covered with plywood because there were only two workers. A Sunday morning appeal turned out ten workers that afternoon, and the plywood went on. When some complained that only a few were doing most of the work, it was realized that some were working on the building, some were working on Heifer Project, some were working on the church fair, and some just were not able to work.

Almost all decisions were brought before the whole church. There were votes on paint colors, choice of carpet, and sanctuary arrangement. One particularly good memory lingers. When the sanctuary was nearly done, it was time to put up and finish the wainscoting. Over some objections, it was decided to paint the wainscoting. One of our loyal workers, Ted, proceeded to paint the prime coat. Another member, Emma, who had some interior decorating experience, came in and in her refreshing candor said, "That looks awful!" Her second comment was that if others agreed that natural wood finish would be better, she would help strip the prime coat, since she had "opened her mouth." The decorating committee met, opinions were solicited, discussion went back and forth, and the decision was made to strip. On stripping day, there was outspoken Emma alongside patient Ted, and others of both persuasions, stripping the prime coat together. After the job was finished, all agreed the last decision was the best.

The decorating committee used a small school bus to visit surrounding towns to look at other churches, and the members went to Boston to pick out lighting fixtures. We worshiped in chaos and Sheetrock dust as the work proceeded. The minister pushed for deadlines so church school and the dedication could occur on schedule, and the carpenters resisted. Excitement grew as it became apparent what God, Alice Anderson, many workers, hard work, and cooperation had wrought.

We used our new sanctuary for the first time on Thanksgiving Sunday 1975. It was not quite finished, but it was beautiful! We praised God and gave thanks. Our area minister preached. A "full house" came back in the evening for a rousing hymn sing and a refreshment buffet.

Work continued through the winter on the finishing touches in the new building and on the restoration of the old building. By dedication day, April 25, 1976, we were ready to celebrate. As Charles Morse wrote in his history, "It was a day to be long remembered."[6] Eighty-one people came to worship. Our conference minister and president was present and preached. We dedicated our chapel and the church:

L: For the worship and service of the living God
P: We dedicate this expanded Metcalf Chapel.
L: To be a place for meditation and celebration, confession and thanksgiving, for hearing and responding to the Word, where we can grow closer to our God and neighbor,
P: We dedicate this room.
L: To be a common ground where people of all ages and interests can work and play, learn and grow, accept and be accepted,
P: We dedicate this tool of Your ministry.
L: To be a people reaching out, serving, risking, healing, feeding, helping, loving, growing,
P: We re-dedicate ourselves as Your church in this place.

By the end of Act II, in 1976, we were, like our building, restored and new—still in the same place, but ready for new experiences and challenges. Heifer Project had connected us with the larger world and taught us that our only limitations were those we placed on ourselves. Our building project gave us that attractive, functional space we needed. But even more, we learned again what a gracious God and hardworking people can do together.

ACT III

The beginning of Act III saw the continuation of concerns raised by our involvement in Heifer Project. During Lent there was a hunger study group. A few of our families grew corn for a New England World Food Garden project that was going to harvest a special variety of corn, mill it, and send it to an area of the world where there was a food shortage. For the first time we participated in the Church World Service clothing collection. And a generous offering was collected for Guatemalan earthquake relief.

After a year and a half of intensive church activity, it was time for some rest and recreation. On Pentecost 1976 we celebrated the birthday of the church with an outdoor worship service, climaxed by the release of fifty gas balloons carrying a printed greeting and return address. Worship was followed by a picnic, kite festival, and ball game. The church led the community in a celebration of the national bicentennial weekend with a Saturday steak barbecue and band concert and a colonial worship service with authentic costumes.

We had become a confident, competent, and usually compassionate church. But I sensed something was lacking. In the first sermon of 1976, I sought to articulate my concerns and called for a new direction:

> Over the last year we've grown in numbers and achievements. We've worked very hard. We are a hardworking, loyal, spirited church. Now we need to grow spiritually—in faith, trust, sensitivity, and knowledge; in a sense of mission and responsibility. We've grown wider; now let's grow deeper. . . . I'm calling you to grow toward a risking, adventurous faith. That is going to be the emphasis in my ministry this year.

A deeper faith dimension in our personal and corporate life was the first focus in our third act.

We also needed to change our concept of ministry from what David, the paid minister, does for the church, to what the laity—the whole people of God—do. I gradually realized I was most comfortable and satisfied when I was out in front, organizing the expedition, leading the way, and doing a large share of the work, but it was necessary for my style and the congregation's to change. Neither was going to be easy.

A month after the faith development challenge, I raised a second issue of ministry when we were commissioning our church officers and committee members. I introduced H. Richard Niebuhr's concept that the nature of the professional minister's job is to be a "pastoral director" who trains, encourages, and supports the lay ministers who carry on the church's ministry.[7] Three dimensions of the church's ministry were identified: The laity should learn to minister better to one another within the fellowship of the church; our ministry should include strengthening the church—the institution or organization—so that it could be more effective; and we should prepare laity to exert a penetrating Christian influence on the world through the quality of

22

personal living, social and community involvements, and vocation.

After developing a capable, committed church with an attractive, appropriate building, we were now embarking in Act III on the development of a deeper faithfulness and a more effective life and ministry together.

The key ingredient to our faithfulness-effectiveness emphasis was our involvement in a two-year pilot program at The Hartford Seminary Foundation. I wanted to do some concentrated reflection on ministry in small churches and I had heard that Hartford was initiating a unique doctor of ministry degree program, which included a component involving the pastor's parish. I shared the program and my own excitement with our moderator and our Church Committee. After a Hartford representative interpreted the program to the church, the membership voted to participate.

The "parish development" aspect of the program included a computerized before-and-after parish survey, a "Coordinating Committee" to administer the program in the parish, a Hartford consultant to assist us through the two years, and five courses or consultations with Hartford faculty in our church. Our state conference agreed to pay half the church's tuition. We were one of seven New England and New York State churches from four denominations accepted for the new program.

An article in the *Athol Daily News*, a nearby newspaper, asked, "It is not unusual for a minister to go back to school to do post-graduate study, but who ever heard of a whole church going to seminary for two years, without ever leaving home?"[8] The emphasis in the program was that which I had raised several months earlier—development of a commitment to a mutual ministry and learning how to be a more faithful and effective church.

The parish survey was probably the most helpful aspect of the whole program. We used an intensive process to present the findings to the church, to elicit their reactions and ideas, and then to use the data and the ideas and priorities of our people to set some two-year goals and to select the appropriate Hartford courses for our church. By looking at the data and talking with one another, we discovered that we knew ourselves and one another better, that we really cared about our church and community, that we wanted assistance in specific areas, and that we wanted our church to be more than it was.

Specifically, the survey indicated and discussion verified that—

- Our church shared a strong sense of community, the morale of our membership was high, we shared a sense of excitement about our future, and there was a high level of commitment.
- We needed help in the areas of spiritual growth, Christian education, and mission.
- We were satisfied with our worship and sense of caring and community.

As we proceeded toward setting some goals for ourselves, we used two principles advocated by our Hartford consultant. The first was that goals should be selected which both correct weaknesses *and* build on strengths. Groups usually focus only on weaknesses, which tends to be self-defeating. Who wants to spend all the time looking at problems and failures? There will be more energy for working on goals if some of the effort is concentrated on utilizing strengths as well as addressing areas of weakness. The second principle was that goals should focus both on the tasks of the church (e.g., worship, education) and on the processes of the church (e.g., communication, planning, morale).

The various committees in the church were asked to take the findings from the survey, the discussions that had transpired, and their own priorities and develop three or four goals or projects their particular committee wanted to concentrate on over the next two years. The resulting goals of each group were brought to a church meeting for revision and adoption. Out of a total of seventeen, nine were achieved and progress was made on five more. These goals did move us a long way toward our dreams without restricting us. They gave the groups a focus beyond maintenance of the status quo. They helped the groups be more accountable to the congregation. As we pursued them we felt a sense of progress. The goals helped us establish priorities. Work on the goals led to what we had hoped for—a more profound sense of faith and community within the church, a more efficient and productive church organization, and a significant impact on the town, which changed its perception of our church.

Out of our goal process came three new programs that were of particular importance to both church and community. The first was the Warwick Community Newsletter. Four years before, while I was working as part-time coordinator of a four-town community self-help organization, a newsletter containing local and area news was developed and mailed to each home in the four towns. It was a valuable vehicle of communication. When the organization disbanded for lack of support, we looked for an organization in each town to continue this newsletter.

Our church agreed to sponsor the Warwick newsletter. The newsletter was particularly important for Warwick, since there was no radio station or newspaper that reached even a majority of the homes in the community. The format was separate church and town sections. Volunteers were found to gather information, write copy, type stencils, mimeograph, and collate. It goes out monthly, free of charge, to every home in town and to college students, people in the military, friends, and relatives. It is paid for by money budgeted by the church and from donations from community organizations, individuals, and out-of-town subscribers. As a result of the newsletter there is greater participation in town and church events and a greater awareness of town business and activity. People look forward to receiving it and it is a monthly reminder of the church's commitment to serving the community.

The second significant project that developed is our Helping Hands emergency services project. Warwick, like most small towns, is justifiably proud of its tradition of neighbors helping neighbors, yet it was clear that needs often went unmet. The Warwick grapevine was not nearly as effective as people assumed. People did not want to "burden" others. New people did not know whom to call. In many cases Yankee independence resulted in needless want and worry. And people willing to help did not know how to help.

Out of the initial survey and a "Caring for Persons" Hartford course came the decision to develop a hotline tailored to the unique nature and needs of a community of five hundred. A mother-daughter team agreed to coordinate it. Volunteers provided such emergency services as transportation, meals, baby-sitting, and housing. While the number of people using Helping Hands has not been overwhelming, it has filled a real need in our community and again communicated the concern of the church for the community.

The third significant change that grew out of the survey and the Hartford program was in our education program. Our Christian education effort had been evolving since 1971. When I arrived, two or three teachers would disappear into the back room with up to a dozen children for Sunday school. Teachers received no training, assistance, or support. The two or three classes in one room were cold, cramped, and chaotic. Teachers had to spend too much time trying to keep the children quiet so they wouldn't disturb "church" one thin door away or the "class" six feet away. I was not able to use my interest and knowledge about education with teachers or children. And the teachers, who are the people who most need the nourishment of worship, could not worship. Various modifications and alternatives were implemented.

As our Christian Education Committee began to formulate goals in response to the survey, we decided to develop a two-hour Sunday morning with an education hour for all ages and a worship hour with child care for our younger children. The church agreed to try it. A staff of able, loving teachers was recruited, materials were acquired, and the program was publicized. It was a one-year commitment. We are in our fifth year with our two-hour Sunday morning and are very pleased with it. There is more and better learning. Adults are involved. Our teachers can worship. Families and generations can participate together. There is carry-over from what happens in church school to what happens in worship.

While we worked at our goals, five Hartford faculty made the 180-mile round trip to Warwick to teach, preach, lead, and encourage us on our personal and corporate pilgrimages. One course helped us envision what we might be and do as the people of God engaged in a mutual ministry. "Caring for Persons" helped us explore what it means to care for others and be cared for and how we might be a more caring church. A dynamic lay worship leader helped us experience how worship can truly be "the work of the people" (the meaning of the word liturgy). An organizational dynamics person worked with us on ways to make the organization of the church an effective vehicle for being what we are called to be, rather than a roadblock that stymies, discourages, and repels. And finally, Walter Wink, a well-known Bible-study leader, spent a weekend with us doing Bible study for human transformation. By the time he left we had risked, cried, laughed, broken bread together, and discovered a wealth in the Word and in one another. Each time there was a course, a different combination of twelve to twenty people participated. During and beyond this time, I was doing course work at Hartford and developing insights and skills for my ministry in Warwick.

Our involvement with Hartford Seminary was an important phase in our movement as a church. This is illustrated by one section of the follow-up survey conducted in our church in January 1979. People were asked to assess lay involvement prior to 1977 and in 1979. The question read:

Which one of the following statements best describes lay involvement in your congregation/parish before your minister began his Doctor of Ministry Program (January 1977). Which statement best describes it currently?

Before (1977)		Current (1979)
36%	There are a few very active lay people, but most of the parishioners are Sunday-morning onlys.	13%
44%	There are several committees in the church which are active, but no more than half of the congregation are involved other than on Sunday mornings.	10%
16%	There is an active, interested majority of members of this congregation who are involved in worship, educa-	60%

tion, committees and in programs of
the church and in ministering to
one another.

4%   Most members experience the con-   18%
gregation as a support group for
their own ministries to one another,
to the community, to the nation,
and to the world.

This response illustrates a significant change in the church's
self-perception. The congregation came to see itself as a caring, committed community of faith. Ours has become a church
for which small does not mean weak or inferior, for which
a problem is not a threat but a challenge and opportunity,
and for which the future seems open and inviting.

The year 1979 marked our 150th birthday as a church.
While there were celebrations throughout the year, the
highlight was our mid-June anniversary service. Many things
made the day special. Earlier in the year we had purchased
some water- and fire-damaged pews for ten dollars each.
Many men and women worked hard stripping the old finish
and painting and varnishing the pews. The Sunday prior to
the anniversary service, one member said in worship that
it was unrealistic to have them ready for the next Sunday.
Another said we could have them ready if we wanted to.
They were ready and in place the day before the service.
Our already attractive meeting room was transformed. Our
new conference minister and president came to preach and
help baptize our five-month-old son, Aaron. Worshipers came
dressed in clothing from various historical periods. Recalling
1 Peter 2:10, we proclaimed as part of our Call to Worship:
"Once we were no people—now we are God's people. Once
we were no church—now we are God's church. Come let us
worship the God who brought us here and will lead us on!"

Following the sermon, we used the beginning of the 350-
year-old Salem (Mass.) Covenant as part of our pledge for
the future: "We covenant with the Lord and with one another to walk together in all God's ways." And we pledge to
be faithful, just, forgiving, and caring as God leads us into
a new era in our history as the Trinitarian Congregational
Church of Warwick Amen."

Three acts and almost a decade later this is a different

church. We are still on a pilgrimage, but we are much farther down the road. People continue to join us. We have begun gearing up for a variety of initiatives which may include new mission programs, more building expansion, more lay ministry, and becoming a small-church training center

Ours is not a perfect church. We have our disagreements. We are sometimes lazy and complacent. We are often slow to believe and hesitant to act. Feelings are sometimes hurt and people are sometimes forgotten. We are a human and therefore sinful church, like any other.

But things are different in Warwick. God is using this church in exciting ways. Morale is high. We have remained small, while still growing. We are having a significant, positive impact on our town and are taking seriously the larger world. The church is influencing important personal growth in people. Laity are more and more sharing in a mutual ministry with me and assuming a greater share of the leadership responsibility. While still composed of "average" people, this church is even now more remarkable.

Why go to this length to describe one decade in the life of one small, hill-town church? I am convinced that the transformation which occurred here can occur in *any* other small church that is

- willing to work together
- willing to commit itself to a faithful vision
- willing to set out in pursuit of that vision
- willing to utilize all the resources available to it
- and willing to go where the Spirit of God leads

We offer our experience to you as an illustration not of how to do it but of what is possible for other small churches. Some of the principles utilized here, such as the ten commandments for small-church revitalization (pp. 10-15), are transferable to other situations. While I cannot provide you with a specific travel itinerary, I will try to help you plan your pilgrimage, suggest some provisions to take or pick up along the way, point out some pitfalls, recommend some scenic highlights, and offer you encouragement. If you follow along, you will discover that your small vehicle is spirited, peppy, economical, and plenty large. *Bon Voyage! And Godspeed!*

CHAPTER 2

what is a small church?

The big, multihundred twentieth-century Protestant church is a deviation from what has been the typical church throughout church history. If one researched the history of an institution and discovered that for 95 percent of its history it had a single primary shape and nature, and then during one 5 percent segment of its history the institution developed a very different and dominating shape and nature, the researcher would be justified in calling that different form a deviation from the norm. Until this century, one thought of a "church" as an organization of up to 150 people, except for the minority of center-city and "cathedral" churches.

> History is on the side of the small church. Bigness is the new kid on the block. Historically, Protestant denominations in the United States have been comparatively small. At the time of the Civil War, the size of the average Protestant church was less than one hundred members. A few large churches were in the center of the city, or at the center of the ethnic community. By the turn of the century, the average congregation still had less than one hundred fifty members.[1]

It is no wonder that Christian churches have almost always been small, for as Kirkpatrick Sale says, humankind through the long eons of evolution has "had more experience with the small community than any other form and has learned to live in groups of that size more sucessfully than any other."[2]

WHY LARGE CHURCHES?

Yet today, while a majority of American churches are still statistically small, most American church members are in statistically large churches. Fifteen percent of the largest churches reach 50 percent of American church members, and 50 percent of the smallest churches serve 15 percent of the members.[3] Why the shift? Why is the "successful" twentieth-century church the large, multiprogrammed church? There are at least six reasons.

1. In the twentieth century the United States became an urban and centralized nation rather than rural and dispersed. In 1790 some 95 percent of America was rural. The 1920 census showed that for the first time America was an urban nation—54.3 million urban, 51.8 million rural. (It should be noted that the 1970s marked a reversal in this trend, as urban population declined and rural population increased.) Urbanization meant that many rural churches shriveled and new suburban and center city churches thrived. With the centralization of population came the centralization of institutions—government, business, education, and religion. Throughout this century it has been generally assumed and accepted that centralization, whether into corporate conglomerates, regional schools, or centralized churches, was natural, logical, and desirable. This assumption is now being questioned.

2. A second twentieth-century factor was the revolution in transportation. American institutions changed radically when horsedrawn carriages gave way to horseless carriages, trolleys, buses, and subways. Once people had motorized transportation, supermarkets replaced the corner grocery, district schools replaced neighborhood schools, and large preacher- and program-centered churches replaced the neighborhood and family church. Today a fleet of buses and a full parking lot are signs of a "successful" church.

3. Then there was the communications revolution. The development of amplification meant that more people could hear the preacher and sanctuaries could be larger. The development of radio and television meant that the religionist who mastered the media captured the multitudes. The

print, audio, and visual revolutions changed the dominant concept of communication from interpersonal interaction and exchange to personal reception and assimilation. The style of communication mastered by the small church—the interpersonal—became an anachronism. One result of the transportation and communications revolutions was a shift from high commitment to low commitment on the part of participants. Author E.F. Schumacher notes that "a highly developed transport and communications system has one immensely powerful effect: it makes people footloose."[4] This is true not only in culture but also in church.

4. An important factor in the development of large churches was the simultaneous growth of denominational structures. Winthrop Hudson observes, "By 1900 most of the denominations had begun to assume direct responsibility for many activities previously carried on by voluntary societies."[5] Much that denominations now do in such areas as missions and education was done by specialized societies and agencies. According to Presbyterian official Richard Hutcheson Jr., "The development of corporatized denominational structures is a 20th century phenomenon. It did not reach full flower until after World War II."[6] Is it only coincidence that the growth of churches occurred with the growth and centralization of denominational structures?

Once the purpose of the denomination was to be the servant of the local congregation (at least in the free church tradition). It was expected to provide resources for like-minded churches. It was to assist local churches in the development, maintenance, and placement of learned and doctrinally orthodox clergy. The denomination was a switchboard facilitating interchurch communications. But clearly when one thought "church," one thought of the local church and not national and international denominations. Like the large congregation, the denomination has become a multiprogram, corporatized institution.

There are many virtues to a powerful denominational structure, but there are also dangers. More than ever the denominational tail is wagging the local church dog, rather than the dog wagging the tail. For example, denominational official Paul Madsen seems to give the denomination the

32

right to make life-and-death decisions for the dependent (and small) church:

> If strategy indicates that a local church should change its ministry or even close its doors, there should be a calm acceptance that the kingdom of God demands sacrifice and the willingness to lose our lives that others might find it. . . . There are "core churches," too, that are essential for denominational and interdenominational strategy. . . . "Core churches" must be identified and supported to full and vital life.[7]

Whether the denomination has assumed or been given its vastly greater responsibilities, and whether or not a corporatized structure is the best means to accomplish the tasks, the result is that it takes more money to pay for them and larger local churches to fulfill the denomination's program expectations. It is in the interest of the denomination for the local church to be large, affluent, and generous. Contemporary denominations need large churches to pay for the denominational superstructure.

5. A fifth factor is that local churches need many people to pay for their own superstructures. The Episcopal Church came up with the guideline that "for a parish to be economically healthy, it must have a budget of $60,000 with two hundred active communicants."[8] Ministers have recognized that a church of five hundred can and will pay a larger salary than a church of one hundred. Lay people have recognized that a member in a church of five hundred will not need to contribute as much as a member in a church of one hundred. Ministers and churches together have realized that a church of five hundred can afford more building, more staff, more resources, and more niceties than a church of one hundred. Hence it has made economic sense to many churches to sacrifice intimacy for solvency. In the definition of what a church should be, cost-effectiveness criteria now rival expectations of community, mission, and discipleship. Many smaller churches are trying to compete in an ecclesiastical version of an arms race that they can never win.

6. Finally, size has become synonymous with success, because the church has accepted the cultural assumption that bigger is better. Schumacher writes, "Today, we suffer

from an almost universal idolatry of giantism."[9] Winthrop Hudson chronicles how in the 1920s, churches responded to societal pressures and competition with snappy slogans and promotional stunts:

> "A friendly church" became a familiar slogan which compared favorably with more flashy punch-lines such as "Be a Sport—Come to Church" or the hard-sell "Worship Increases Your Efficiency" and "Business Success and Religion Go Together." Catchy sermon topics—"The Irishmen of the Old Testament," "Two in a Bed," "The Mae West of My Bible"—were used as teasers to draw a crowd.[10]

This kind of hucksterism did not die in the 1920s. The twentieth-century church has read Jesus' commission to "go . . . to all peoples . . . and make them my disciples [Matt. 28:19, TEV]," and has understood it to mean "make them all members of a few large churches."

The first question one pastor will ask another as they compare churches is "how large is your church?" There is no question that in most religious circles the bigger church is considered the better church. Therefore, many small churches, in order to measure up, have become big churches. When a church gets large enough to measure up, however, it usually stops growing.

DIFFERENT UNDERSTANDINGS OF "SMALL CHURCH"

While most churches would prefer to be larger, the majority of American churches are small. In reading about small churches, one soon discovers different understandings of what "small" is. Following are several criteria that Lyle Schaller and others use to define what is a small church.[11]

1. The favorite criterion is number of members. Two hundred is the number most use to distinguish small from medium. Therefore, 65 percent of American Baptist, 62 percent of United Methodist and the Disciples of Christ, 52 percent of United Presbyterian, and 51 percent of United Church of Christ churches are "small." The Presbyterian Church U.S. reports that 72 percent of its churches have fewer than 250 members. Of Protestant denominations, only the Southern Baptists, the American Lutheran Church, and

the Lutheran Church in America reported fewer than 50 percent of their churches in the two hundred or less category, and their percentages were all over 40 percent.[12]

2. Worship attendance is another criterion. One third of all Protestant churches have fewer than seventy-five at their morning worship. Some would consider this an indicator of a small church. It is probably a more reliable standard than relying on membership totals, since these numbers do not give an accurate picture of how many people are actively participating.

3. When a congregation recalls a past when they were larger, they call themselves small. A church that once had a thousand members and now has four hundred will think of itself as small. There are great empty spaces in the sanctuary, red ink on the ledger, and a sense of inadequacy.

4. When churches are compared, the smaller is often considered small (even if it does not fit the statistical criteria). Schaller quotes a thirty-two-year-old pastor of a 385-member congregation: "I grew up in a big congregation, I served my intern year while in seminary in a 2,100 member parish, and after graduation I spent five years as an associate in a 1,700 member church. It takes awhile to get used to being in a small church with all of its limitations."[13]

5. The size of the building is sometimes used to determine the size of the church. The little white New England church, which happens to be full, is a small church. The large center-city church building with a sparse congregation is seldom thought of as a small church.

6. The bottom line on size is often the budget. "In the 1970s (1974), we would now estimate $25,000 as the minimum for congregational survival, and $40,000 necessary for real effectiveness."[14] How high should these figures be in the 1980s to cover inflation? For many, money is the real criterion of what is and is not a small church.

7. A full workload is sometimes considered the transition point between small and medium. Schaller quotes a denominational official who suggested, "Another rule of thumb is widely used that each minister should serve a congregation with 300 to 350 members before that can be considered a full-time workload."[15]

8. Carl Dudley suggests that the characteristic of caring is basic to the definition of a small church. "Small churches are a single, caring cell embracing the whole congregation."[16] Larger churches have several caring groups divided according to age, interest, or task. A small church is one large clanlike caring group.

9. The number and variety of fellowship circles or primary face-to-face groups are factors used in categorizing churches. It is assumed that large churches will have a variety of programming opportunities for all ages to meet many needs and to satisfy many interests. On the other hand, a church with a limited program is considered small.

Small churches may be found anywhere, but they are more likely to be in small-town and rural settings. Up-to-date statistics are hard to find, but the 1936 census of religious bodies revealed that the average urban church at that time had 541 members, compared to an average of 143 for rural churches. In a 1965 study of Methodist churches, Methodist churches in communities of less than 2,500 averaged 128 members, those in communities between 2,500 and 10,000 averaged 475 members, and those in communities over 10,000 averaged 660 members.[17] In a 1978 survey conducted of United Church of Christ small churches in Massachusetts, I discovered that two thirds of the churches are in small towns and rural areas. However, with the out-migration from cities and the development of ethnic and nondenominational churches, there are a growing number of urban small churches.

Church planner Douglas Walrath has done some significant research on the types and contexts of small congregations. He contends that one cannot understand a small church unless one has identified (1) its social context, (2) its social position, and (3) the type of congregation.[18] First, Walrath suggests that there are twelve types of social contexts—Midtown, Inner City, Inner-Urban, Outer-Urban, City Suburb, Metropolitan Suburb, Fringe Suburb, Fringe Village, Fringe Settlement, Independent City, Rural Village, and Rural Settlement—and that each locale has a characteristic church which is a logical extension of its setting and the people likely to be in that setting.

Social position, the church's "posture" in relation to the surrounding community or neighborhood, is the second method Walrath uses to understand churches. There are three essential social types: Dominant, Subordinate, and Exclusive. The Dominant church is the prestige church, the large church, the oldest, the wealthiest, the one with the most powerful people. The Subordinate church is the "other" church, the one in the shadow of or down the block from the Dominant church. The third type is the Exclusive church. It is exclusive because it addresses a specific identity, need, or interest; it may be the ethnic church, the house church, the church dominated by one or a few families, or the conservative church with rigid theological and social requirements.

The third way Walrath looks at churches is as one of five types of organization. Most typical is the Independent church, which has its own pastor or staff and is programmatically on its own. The Yoked church shares a minister with one or more congregations. Walrath considers the Yoke the weakest and yet the most popular interchurch relationship. Team ministry describes a situation in which two or more ministers cooperate in serving two or more congregations. This is becoming more viable as husband-and-wife teams are seeking to work together. In a Cluster, two or more congregations cooperate when it comes to program. Clusters are generally more satisfying to pastors and congregations. Finally, there is the Cluster-Team, which combines a team of ministers and more than one church working together in both staffing and programming. While it offers the most potential, it requires the most organizational maintenance.[19]

Effective small-church planning requires that all three of these factors be identified and consideration given to the way they will interface.

Small churches can be defined and analyzed statistically, economically, historically, ecclesiastically, geographically, and sociologically. Another way to look at them is psychologically. Lowery and Dudley have indicated that the bottom line for the small church is economics. But there is another bottom line—self-image. A negative self-image is a terminal illness in many small churches. Sometimes it stems from a threatening environment, sometimes from a form of internal cancer, and sometimes from malnutrition. Frequently a poor self-image has been transmitted by outside experts and authorities as well as by society's stifling sizism (see Introduction, p. xiv).

Paul Madsen identifies five reasons small churches are small: an inadequate program, an inadequate field (limited population to draw on), an inadequate evangelism, an inadequate vision, and inadequate personalities.[20] Apparently if the situation in each of these areas had not been inadequate, these churches would be adequate, normal, and *large*. Any small church that accepts these as the reasons for its size is sure to feel defeated.

Small size is especially a problem for small urban and suburban churches. It is much harder to feel worthy or adequate when the church up the avenue has twice as many members, double the staff, a larger budget and salaries, and a commanding presence. In rural areas the small church is rarely in the shadow of larger embodiments of ecclesiastical success; it is either the only church in town or else all the churches are small.

The self-image a church has is often determined by the kind and quality of ministerial leadership. Much of the ministerial leadership in our smaller churches has been uninspiring and inadequate, but many highly competent pastors have chosen to serve small churches. The title of a recent book, *Send Us a Minister . . . Any Minister Will Do*, by Walter Cook of Bangor (Me.) Theological Seminary, poignantly illustrates the despair many small churches have felt as they sought pastoral leadership. Five negative but prevalent pastoral settlement images have helped shape the self-image of many small churches:

- Proving Grounds: These are the small churches where fledgling ministers go to get their feet wet, their appetites stimulated, their eyes opened, and their skills sharpened so they can move on to bigger and better things.
- Siberia: These are the churches on the fringe where

seminaries and denominations consign ministers who cannot make it in the mainstream.

- Pasture: These are the warm, cozy pastorates where aging pastors go to await retirement or to supplement an inadequate pension.
- Heinz Soup Factory (57 varieties): These are the small, struggling churches where ministers from unaccredited Bible colleges or diploma mills work for any amount of money and often take the church for a ride out of its denomination and heritage.
- Bargain Basement: These churches can get more minister than they can pay for because they are the homes of surplus ministers.

Unfortunately, negative self-images become self-fulfilling prophecies. A church that does not expect to find quality leadership will generally not find it. A church that does not feel desirable is apt to find itself with undesirable leadership. But how will that negative self-image be reversed if no one offers a positive one?

SMALL IS A BIBLICAL VIRTUE

The Bible is a biased book. One does not have to read far in the Law, the Prophets, the Gospels, and the Epistles to discover a special concern for the poor, the dispossessed, the disadvantaged, the righteous, and the young. Another bias appears to be a special appreciation for the small. In the Old Testament, whenever society grew large it grew out of control. In the first eleven chapters of the Bible, God twice saw that it was necessary to start over with smaller groupings—once with Noah and his family and then again when all the people tried to settle in one large city around the tower of Babel. At the end of Genesis, Jacob divided Israel into twelve smaller units, with one of his sons as leader of each tribe.

The history of Israel is a cyclic saga of God's people growing large, prosperous, and unfaithful and then declining with a small, faithful remnant emerging, only to repeat the cycle. Deuteronomy 7:7-8 records God's bias for small

Israel: "It was not because you were more in number than any other people that the Lord set his love upon you and chose you, for you were the fewest of all peoples; but it is because the Lord loves you."

The stories of David and Goliath, and Gideon and the Midianites, are two illustrations of God's using smallness. The story of David and Goliath (1 Samuel 17) is not a rejection of bigness or a glorification of smallness, but a tribute to faithfulness. Because of David's faithfulness his size was no handicap; indeed, it was an advantage, because it enabled David to catch Goliath off guard. The story also illustrates God's propensity for acting in unlikely ways.

The story of Gideon and the Midianites (Judges 7) recognizes the human propensity for presumptuousness. Because of Israel's sinfulness they were occupied by the Midianites. Israel then cried for help, and Gideon was appointed their liberator. Gideon fearfully pleaded, "How can I deliver Israel? Behold, my clan is the weakest in Manasseh and I am the least in my family." God cut him short with, "But I will be with you." Gideon recruited an army of 32,000. Probably recalling past behavior, God recognized that if Israel prevailed over Midian with 32,000 soldiers they would "vaunt themselves" against God saying, "My own hand has delivered me." God proceeded to winnow the 32,000 down to 300, and this remnant army prevailed and the Midianites were routed. Part of God's bias for the small is a result of the tendency for the big to become gods unto themselves. The small must rely on grace more than on clout.

The prophets, and particularly Isaiah, speak of the faithful remnant among the faithless. "For though your people Israel be as the sand of the sea, only a remnant of them will return [Isa. 10:22]." Repeatedly throughout scripture God affirms the few, the small, the insignificant. With rare exceptions, biblical faithfulness does not come from or result in large numbers. God is willing to spare Sodom and Gomorrah if ten righteous people can be found, Christ is present where two or three gather in his name, the widow's mite is the largest gift, and the boy with a few loaves and fish provides the food for thousands. The mustard seed, the pearl of great price, the lost sheep and coin, the sparrows and the numbered hairs are all powerful small images of promise.

And consider the incarnation. The messianic expectation was for a royal, mighty, divine being who would liberate, judge, and rule forever. The realization of the incarnation was something else. Scripture tells us that Jesus was born in a stable to a blue-collar couple, raised in a disreputable town, and carried on an unassuming itinerate town and country ministry with the aid of a dozen nondescript followers. The gospel Jesus preached and practiced stressed intimacy, personal and communal relationships, and attention to individual needs and gifts. He did not build institutions or encourage mass movements. His person-to-person ministry culminated in an ignoble death. Jesus the Christ came and went as a commoner. Even the resurrection appearances were not the media events one might expect, but rather encounters in a garden, on a road, and behind closed doors. The Savior of the world was most at home in small groups and had a special affinity for the simple, the unlikely, and the insignificant.

The small church can easily develop an inferiority complex when it measures itself by contemporary standards of success. If it chooses to measure itself by biblical criteria, however, it may find itself being affirmed, worthy, legitimate. Its small size does not guarantee legitimacy, but it cannot be the criteria for damnation or ridicule. Size has nothing to do with the biblical marks of the church. Is the word heard and are the sacraments kept? Are love and justice preached and practiced? Is the Christ incarnated in word and deed? Does the body expend itself in redemptive action? Size is irrelevant to biblical faithfulness and effectiveness.

There have been many attempts to define "small church." Most have been negative—what it is not, what it cannot do, what it cannot be. They have tended to reinforce inferiority complexes, rather than offer a vision of what is possible for them. Most have focused on the limits of numbers—people and dollars. While defining the small church by its size, they have not recognized in any careful way the particular implications of size—either large or small. They have identified the small church by statistics more than by personality, function, and potential. What follows is a more complete and fruitful understanding of "small church" described in terms of what it naturally is, can be, and can do.

A DIFFERENT DEFINITION OF "SMALL CHURCH"

As we all know, a big mansion is not simply a bungalow with more rooms, a big party is not simply an intimate dinner with more people, a big metropolitan hospital is not simply a clinic with more beds and more doctors, a big corporation is not simply a family firm with more employees and products, a big government is not simply a town council with more branches.

Size, indeed, might well be regarded as *the* crucial variable in anything.[21]

Georg Simmel, turn-of-the-century pioneer German sociologist, broke fresh ground by researching and writing about the significance of size in the way groups function. That ground has seldom been turned since. While it might seem obvious that a city of 100,000 will function and interact differently from a town of 1,000, or a church of 1,000 will feel and act differently from a church of 100, few have tried to determine the nature of the difference. Amos Hawley wrote:

It is a matter of common knowledge that as the size of the social aggregate increases the behavior of its members changes. . . . But we have little precise knowledge of the relation between size of population and organization. Apparently the relation has been so taken for granted that it has not been thought worthy of careful investigation. Yet size of population is doubtlessly one of the most limiting factors in man's collective life.[22]

But size of population is also one of the most enabling factors in group life.

The small church is *not* a prepubescent, immature, dwarfed, or malnourished large church. Because of its different size and resulting different nature, it is a uniquely different species. It will look different, feel different, act differently, be different. It is the differences that make the definition. Small churches are different from their larger ecclesiastical cousins in at least ten essential ways:

1. *The small church is the common expectations of its members.* It is different because members and visitors expect it to be different. One's expectations of an organization go a long way toward determining the reality of the organization. People expect greater informality, intimacy, immediacy, personal attention, and involvement in small churches. People who are attracted by those qualities will gravitate toward the places where they expect to find them. People desiring formality or anonymity will seek out places where those expectations can be met. People who are unhappy in small churches probably have large-church expectations. Thus we have a self-fulfilling prophecy. Because we have a common expectation, we seek to realize those expectations.

People also have some negative expectations of small churches. Frequently they expect to find less able leadership and poor-quality programming. If poor leadership, a weak education program, and shoddy worship are expected, they will be too readily accepted as inevitable.

2. *The small church is one where almost everyone knows everyone.* Author A. Paul Hare observes, "A group is usually defined as 'small' if each member has the opportunity for face-to-face interaction with all others."[23] In a small church, people expect to know one another's business, and they usually do. What is more, they want to know about one another. They are not just being polite when they ask, "How are you?"

This knowledge of one another is crucial, because people behave differently and feel differently with people they know. When we are with people we do not know we are likely to be reserved, lonely, less committed, and ready to flee. On the other hand, if we know one another we tend to feel relaxed, more committed, at home; masks are less common, or at least more transparent. When we know one another, we also know how to hurt the other, but it is more likely that we will care for and stand by one another.

Often a person in a small church will know more people than another person in a larger church. Dudley has observed:

> In larger congregations, the subgroups are considerably larger: 30 to 40 members of a fellowship, 15 to 20 members of a study group or committee, 8 to 10 people for intimate sharing or a prayer cell. But in the small church everyone knows, or knows about, each other. It is a single cell of caring Christians. If the church has a long association with a piece of land and a particular cultural group, it may embrace 200—perhaps 300 or more—people who know each other personally, by family, name and place in the community.[24]

People in growing small churches (or small churches that are resistant to growing) are frequently worried that if they grow they will lose this sense of intimacy. What is often not realized is that whether this happens is determined by such factors as theology, architecture, style, and strategies. A church that stresses only the God-person relationship and downplays the neighbor-to-neighbor relationship will not be an intimate church. A church building with a long, narrow sanctuary and little or no space for mingling and moving about will not be an intimate church. A church with a worship and meeting style that encourages and gives time to community-building and sharing will have a high degree of intimacy. A church that thinks creatively about strategies to help new members and old know one another can remain "small" as it grows. In this regard there are congregations of three hundred that are still small.

3. *The small church is one, not only where most people know each other but also where there is a sense of "family,"* or what the social scientists call a "primary group," in contrast to a "secondary group." Most churches will have one or more primary groups. In many larger churches there will be a primary group composed of those who are the decision-makers and permission-givers, but beyond them the others in the congregation will look and feel like spectators at a participation sport. In other larger churches, members will come together in a variety of primary groups

composed of people of common ages or interests, but the large church as a whole will function as a secondary group. In contrast, one of the characteristics of a small church is that virtually all are part of one common family or primary group. The small-church primary group or familial clan will be a mosaic of ages, interests, abilities, and commitments.

The primary or family group meets three needs people have. First, it gives identity. People have a name and a responsibility. They are recognized when they are there and missed when they are not. Second, it gives people security. They belong and have a voice. They expect the church to be dependable. As one of our members said, "If you need a favor, you don't feel hesitant to ask because you know someone will be happy to help." Third, it is what Dudley means by the "caring cell." People do care about one another.

Also, like families, the primary group can be petty, ingrown, and fractious. Charles Cooley summarizes his feelings about primary groups: "They are not always pleasant or righteous, but they almost always contain elements from which ideals of pleasantness and righteousness may be formed."[25] He adds:

> Christianity, as a social system, is based upon the family, its ideals being traceable to the domestic circle of a Judean carpenter. God is a kind father; man and woman are brothers and sisters; we are all members one of another, doing as we would be done by and referring all things to the rule of love. In so far as the church has departed from these principles it has proved transient; these endure because they are human.[26]

4. *A small church is one where almost everyone feels and is important and needed.* Almost everyone has a feeling of ownership. It has been demonstrated that the members of small churches are more regular in attendance and are more faithful in giving. Georg Simmel recognized decades ago that "The contribution of each to the whole and the group's reward to him are visible at close range; comparison and compensation are easy. In the large group they are difficult."[27]

A strong laity is crucial in a small church. Through much of the Warwick church's history, lay people did all the work, except leading worship, and were responsible for keeping the church alive and functioning. Large churches with full-time and multiple staffs and large budgets can hire people to do the work; small churches cannot afford that.

In the small church the whole membership can come close to fulfilling Ephesians 4:16 (TEV): "Under his control all the different parts of the body fit together, and the whole body is held together by every joint with which it is provided." One of our members recalls her experience in a large Long Island church: "I never had a chance to find out what I could do. . . . You didn't get asked to do the jobs unless you joined the groups. . . . That was never a comfortable place for me to be. My place was on the fringe." She is one of our most valued and capable lay leaders.

5. *A small church is one where group functioning is simple* rather than complex. Organizations work differently depending on the number of people represented in the decision-making and workings of the organization. The more people there are, the more complex their interactions will be. In a small church everyone can have a direct voice in decision-making. Frequently decisions can be worked through until a genuine consensus is reached. People participate directly, rather than indirectly. People who would seethe silently in a church meeting of two hundred will speak out before thirty. All the significant decisions in our building construction and restoring program were made by the whole church, in almost every case by consensus.

In a small church, committees and boards can function more as task forces than as decision-making bodies. They meet, talk, develop tentative plans, and then can come to the whole congregation for a decision, support, and assistance. Rather than act on behalf of the church, subgroups can lead the whole church in action.

In a small church, communication is horizontal rather than vertical. People actively communicate with one another, rather than passively receiving messages from the top. Communication is also more immediate. A quick series of phone calls on Saturday got the word to all our homes to wear red or white for a special Pentecost service. The whole body can be informed rather than left out.

When necessary, the small church can be mobilized for quick action. It takes less energy to move small bodies than large ones, and small bodies can move more quickly than bulky, unwieldy ones.

This is not to say there are no criticisms, rumors, and pettiness that travel the grapevine. But they do not go as far and they surface sooner, so the differing parties and views can be brought together for clarification and often reconciliation. It is also easier in a small church for one or two or a handful to stymie or derail the rest. It will not work to ignore the dissenter or nonconformist, he or she must be reckoned with.

6. *The identity of a small church is in its collective personality and experience, rather than in its program.*

> The larger congregation knows who it is because of what it does, and it must keep on doing, in order to reassure its existence. The small church has identity because of the experiences that it brings from the past. Its primary satisfactions are in the relationships among people who share experiences in faith. They find identity in their character, not in their activities.[28]

New people will be attracted or repelled more by the people than by the program. A church with six choirs, a basketball team, a men's club, a great youth program, a nursery school, Bible study groups, and a hospice program can sell its program. A church without the great range of programs can only say "We are who we are, the body of Christ in this place." The beauty of this reality is that rather than competing with the schools, agencies, and community groups to offer the most attractive programs, the small church is free to be what no one else can be—an intimate, caring, faithful people, colored by their own zany, peculiar, intriguing chemistry of history and personality. It is particularly important for a small church to discover what is distinctive about it, so this uniqueness can be highlighted and celebrated.

7. *A small congregation claims a common history and is committed to a common future.* Families share a family history, and the history usually includes legends, skeletons, heroes, humor, pathos, tragedy, and conquest. It is upon this, as it is known, shared, and possessed, that a present is understood and a future is built.

History is uniquely special to small churches because a larger proportion will have a personal tie with the characters and saints, holy moments and symbolic episodes that are the remembered history. In a small church the people know that the maintenance and fulfillment of their shared history is in their hands. In the typical small-church building one is surrounded, as in a museum, by the symbols and artifacts that embody the way it was and the ones who were.

Newcomers do not join an organization. They are adopted into the family or grafted onto the family tree. Whether the adoption or grafting takes depends on whether the newcomer is helped to and chooses to become a descendant in the family line of succession. Dudley believes that the small church will permit itself to grow only at the rate that newcomers can be assimilated.

Jesus said that he came not to abandon the law but to fulfill it. Pity the pastor or newcomer in the small church who seeks to deny, ridicule, or abandon those historical ties. And happy is the pastor or newcomer who is blessed with the wisdom and skill to help the people build on or fulfill their history. Our experience in Warwick has been that there is little resistance to change when the change does not deny or deface our shared history.

The wise new pastor will quickly find out which pictures and places are holy to the people and which have merely appeared without taking on special meaning. Early on I made the mistake of removing a picture of Jesus that had no meaning or appeal for me. Alas, it did have meaning and appeal for others. Today it properly hangs on a mantel overlooking a people and place which have changed and grown considerably while remaining rooted to their solid foundation. "To appreciate the past is not to be bound by it, but to build on it. . . . The small church will die if it loses touch with its history. . . . When the future is constructed from pride in the past, then the richest energy of the small church is released and activated."[29]

8. *In small churches, theology is understood and lived in personal, relational, and historical ways*, more than systematically, academically, or theoretically. Edwin Earp tells of the young seminarian sent to preach in a rural New Hampshire church. Seeing the ground looked bare, he prayed in his pastoral prayer that God send copious showers to quench the thirst of the parched land. After the service was over an old farmer walked up and said, "We had a good rain yesterday; what we need up here just now is not rain, but manure."[30]

The small church that has struggled and survived wants no ethereal speculations. Its religion must be real and practical. Since the members live in personal, long-term relationships with one another, their faith has been learned and experienced in personal and relational terms. God will be met and experienced more on the horizontal plane than the vertical. God is not up there or out there, but among us. Since they are close to their history, they can identify God as being active in that history. The God who was real to the remnant people of the Old Testament makes sense to today's remnant. The God the psalmist found revealed in nature makes sense to our rural people. The Jesus who taught with human stories and pastored along the roadside, around the dinner table, and beside the sickbed is a Christ who makes sense to them. Most likely their clergy have been pastors and shepherds, more than philosophers and speculators. The theology learned from these clergy has been personal and pragmatic. And the theology their clergy preach today had better be as down-to-earth as the old farmer's need for manure.

9. *A small church is one where mission is understood and implemented in personal and immediate terms.* Denominations prefer undesignated mission money to support a wide and diversified mission effort. Perhaps congregations that are wide and diversified do not need to be more specific in interpreting and selling mission than to say the money is for

the "larger mission of the church." However, members of a small church do not get excited about the impersonal approach. They do get excited about helping their neighbor, and if you help them discover a needy neighbor in Brazil or Zaire, they will get excited.

Small churches are often criticized for being survival-oriented rather than mission-oriented, because far more money goes for the pastor's salary and institutional needs than for "mission." However, because a church does not send much money for denominational mission support does not necessarily mean it is concerned only with survival.

Our Warwick church illustrates that when a small church can identify what and where the specific need is and who is being helped, it will respond. The $3,300 raised for Heifer Project is evidence of this. We knew we were supporting our volunteer, buying an acre at the Heifer Project ranch in Arkansas, and buying animals for a specific place. People who deal with one another on a personal basis will respond to a mission challenge if that is on a personal basis. And a personal response can be an attack on a universal problem.

In addition, many small churches carry on significant mission in their local communities. Their buildings are used by community groups. Especially in small communities, the church will have several members serving in local government and volunteering in a variety of community programs. Community newsletters are published. Food co-ops are sponsored. Ministers become pastors for whole communities. Even the rummage sale, bazaar, and fair provide good clothing and merchandise at bargain prices. The small church is a source of help for community people in times of crisis. Small churches that cannot give significant sums of money often make significant "in kind" contributions (e.g., clothing to Church World Service and collections for recycling projects). While they may not be good at going through a sophisticated planning process to develop a sophisticated mission project, they can be good at quickly and effectively meeting human need.

10. *The small church is one where the clergyperson is seen as a person, pastor, and generalist,* not as a stereotype,

specialist, or administrator. The small church frequently expects its minister to be precisely what the seminary often does not train students to be, and it does not want what the seminary often does train ministers to be. In a study of rural clergy, one minister wrote: "Ministers succeed or fail . . . not on their ability to preach, nor on their knowledge of history; not on their Biblical understanding, nor any of the scholarly matters, but on their ability to effectively communicate a Christian concern for people."[31]

A small church with no pretensions or delusions of grandeur will quickly puncture any such pretensions or delusions a minister brings to them. What they want is not a scholar, therapist, manager, or expert, but a member and a leader of the family. This is not to say small churches do not want or need competent and skilled clergy leadership, but these skills will not be responded to until the door to the church's collective soul is opened with warmth, concern, and vulnerability. In a book about seminarians' experiences in small Maine churches, Walter Cook illustrates the relationship between small churches and their pastor:

> I asked him . . . "Why are you attracting a larger attendance than any recent pastor before you?" With a grin he readily acknowledged, "It's sure not because I'm a terrific preacher." When I talked with his church members I found it was because he knows them as friends and is interested in everything about them. They said, "He's always dropping in for a few minutes on somebody. He knows *us*; we know *him*."[32]

Not every numerically small church will possess all of the above ten descriptive, natural marks of an authentically small church. Larger churches may find that some of these shoes fit, but because of the dynamics of size, it would be impossible for them all to fit a church with many people.

These ten distinctive qualities of a small church are not the only ones that can describe a small church. There are also negative qualities often found in smaller churches: coolness to those outside "the family," low self-esteem, defensiveness, acceptance of shoddy programming, parochialism, and a desire merely to survive. Many small churches share with larger churches such qualities as constant conflict, aimlessness, self-satisfaction, and self-absorption. But instead of dwelling on inadequacies, a small church would be better served to look at the ten positive marks of a small church and strive to embody them more fully.

A small church seeking to be more fully what by God's grace it is meant to be would do well to—

- Carefully evaluate itself in relation to the ten distinctive qualities
- Creatively envision the implications and possibilities for itself if it were to capitalize on each quality
- Courageously take concrete steps to incarnate what is uniquely possible for it because of its size

The Christian church has five primary and essential tasks: worship, education, mission, caring for one another, and organizational maintenance (so that it can do the first four tasks). Small churches are by nature the right size effectively and faithfully to do each of these essential tasks. (The things it doesn't do well—support large budgets, buildings, and programs—are incidental to the essential tasks.) The next five chapters discuss each of these tasks in relation to the particularities and possibilities of small churches.

FOR DISCUSSION

1. Reflecting on "Different Understandings of 'Small Church,'" in what ways is your church small?

2. Using Walrath's categories, how would you categorize your church?

3. Does the self-image of your church tend to be negative or positive?

4. Does your church meet the author's ten marks of a small church?

CHAPTER 3

worship: the family reunion of the body of christ

One thing that intrigues me about New England is family reunions. Once a year a family clan will rent a hall or reserve a recreation area and come from miles around to renew common ties. On these occasions family news is updated, babies are welcomed into the family, new spouses are confirmed, departed members are remembered and mourned, feuds are resolved and exacerbated, and various indigenous rituals are observed. At the end of the day, people go home with their roots, identity, and place in the family again established.

In a similar way worship in small churches is a family reunion. Grandparents and grandchildren, moms and dads, aunts and uncles, nieces and nephews, husbands and wives, singles and divorced, related by choice or blood, come together to worship their heavenly Parent, exchange greetings and regrets, receive and pass on good news and bad, baptize and confirm, marry and bury, pray and eat, and practice the rituals that tell them who they are, where they belong, and where they need to go. This familial quality of worship in small churches is one of the unique features of this kind of church.

Miriam Therese Winter makes note of the biblical roots of our worship:

The book of Acts verifies both the Jewish and the Christian aspects of early worship, stating that the first Christians "went as a body to the Temple every day but met in their houses for the breaking of bread" (Acts 2:46, JB), and "they preached every day both in the Temple and in private houses" (Acts 5:42, JB).

She goes on to cite other New Testament passages that tell how early Christians met in the homes of members: Acts 1:13, 12:12, Romans 16:3-5, Colossians 4:15, and Philemon 2.[1] Our worshiping ancestors in the faith came together in extended family-type groups in homes and for several decades worshiped in a style possible and appropriate only for small numbers of people.

Since the time of Vatican II, in both Catholic and Protestant churches, there has been a profound renewal of worship. Serious students and shapers of this renewal effort have gone back to documents from the early church to discover the genius of early worship and a soul for their own. What has generally been overlooked in the search for worship roots is that the small size of those early churches had much to do with the style, content, and distinctiveness of their worship.

When the early Christians came together, they usually worshiped in a member's home or in a simple room, not an imposing sanctuary. Worship began with the "kiss of peace," when *all* the people greeted one another. Their worship was marked by the active participation of all—or at least all the men. Everyone was encouraged to pray, and not just the "president." The preaching or proclamation was specific and maintained a discipline that was necessary for their survival. Their worship was centered around a common meal. Acts tells us that "the company of those who believed were of one heart and soul [Acts 4:32]." When the early church worshiped it really was a liturgy, which means the "work of the people." Five hundred people could not then, and cannot now, worship in this fashion.

Worship in the early church enabled Jew and gentile to discover they had Christ in common, men and women were able to come closer than was otherwise possible in that culture, slaves and owners of slaves found a common bond as they prayed together, the rich shared freely with those in need, and a people made alien in their society by their faith found in their life together a hope and courage to persevere. There was a commonality in early church worship which we have since lost. "There is neither Jew nor Greek, there is neither slave nor free, there is neither male nor female; for you are all one in Christ Jesus [Gal. 3:28]."

> The assertion that the gift of grace is bestowed on *every* church member, and that therefore *every* member is called to service, is constant in the New Testament, just as it is an understood thing that every church member can baptize, or distribute the Lord's Supper, and has the right to speak in any assembly of the Church.[2]

This kind of commonality is most feasible when people come together in limited numbers.

The rediscovery of early church worship has contributed to significant developments in the worship practices of many Catholics and Protestants. Based on that heritage, there are in use several new liturgies which

> illustrate that contemporary liturgical renewal is taking its cue from the period before the church became big, successful, and respectable; before the church's worship had a chance to become pompous, dramatic, and extravagant; before Sunday service degenerated into a preacher/choir performance for a gathering of isolated, passive individuals. Directives for contemporary worship renewal are coming from a church that was then still a family, gathered around a family table, eating a family meal.[3]

In a small church I will probably never be driven to my knees by architectural splendor as I was the first time I entered St. Patrick's Cathedral in New York; I will probably never be stirred by the power and majesty of the music from a great pipe organ, a semi-professional choir, and the unison singing of hundreds of worshipers; I will probably never encounter preaching that overwhelms by the power of amplification, prestige, subtle distance, and feigned intimacy; and I will never have the assurance of being part of a mass movement, which is possible in large churches.

However, in a small church I can experience a sense of

family and community, an awareness of the needs and joys of each organ of the body, a feeling of being cared for by people who really know me, the possibility of worship so finely focused that it is appropriate for most or all the people, the chance for all to rehearse their common future, and the opportunity for each person to participate as an actor in the great drama of worship.

DEFINING WORSHIP AND MAKING IT FIT

There are almost as many definitions of worship as there are worshipers. Evelyn Underhill describes worship as "the response of the creature to the Eternal."[4] James White, one authority on worship, suggests that worship is "the act of standing outside of our normal consciousness in order to become aware of God and to respond."[5] In asking myself the question "What is worship?" I recalled Jesus' great commandment: "You shall love the Lord your God with all your heart, and with all your soul, and with all your mind. . . . You shall love your neighbor as yourself [Matt. 22:37-39]." A helpful definition of worship can be drawn from this familiar admonition. Such a definition would have a multiple focus —on God, neighbor, and ourselves; it would call for a total response—heart, soul, and mind; it would emphasize our active participation—since love is an active verb, rather than a passive feeling; it would connect us with the totality of our lives—home, vocation, leisure, community, world.

According to this definition, worship is the active response of the Christian community to God's love with the praises of our hearts, the yearnings of our souls, and the ponderings of our minds, and the active movement toward a loving mutual ministry to all that are in our sphere of influence. By this definition, an imposing sanctuary, large numbers of people, majestic music, and powerful preaching are not necessary for legitimate worship; in fact, they could be a hindrance. What is necessary is a body of people actively committed to God, to one another, and to a shared ministry beyond the doors of the church.

If worship is the same as liturgy, and if liturgy is the

"work of the people," and if work implies active involvement, how difficult it is for three hundred worshipers to work in the space of one short hour. Individuals in a worshiping body of fifty know that their presence and absence are noticed, that their voices make a difference in the singing and speaking, that their body language is read, that their money in the offering is important, and that a large percentage have a specific responsibility.

Consider a hypothetical small church of fifty worshipers which conscientiously tries to make worship the work of the people. If there are:

- two who are responsible for flowers and decorating
- two who greet and introduce and make welcome
- one who makes and serves coffee and punch
- three children who verbally contribute to the time for children
- two who volunteer announcements
- two ushers chosen randomly from the congregation
- two lay readers
- one who lights the candles and turns up and down the heat
- one who preaches
- thirteen in the youth-adult choir
- ten in the children's choir
- two who accompany the music (in our church we have an organist and a cellist)
- four who voluntarily share concerns during the "time of joys and concerns"

there would be forty-five of fifty worshipers with an active responsibility in the worship experience, in addition to the participation of all the worshipers who share in the corporate prayers, singing, readings, greetings, offering, and spoken reactions. In that church, worship will fulfill Sören Kierkegaard's image of worship as drama in which God is the audience, the congregation are the actors, and the minister is the prompter. Certainly many small congregations have not thought or chosen to involve a high percentage of their worshipers, but they have the potential to do so.

Another significant difference between large and small

churches is that in large churches some will attend worship, some will be in the church school, some in the study groups, some in the social action project, some on the basketball team, and so on, but seldom will they all be together at one time. However, in small churches, worship is the primary and often the only time the church comes together. This fact increases both the opportunity and the responsibility to meet a panorama of needs through worship. Worship is the heart and soul of virtually all small congregations.

Small-church worship is more than a time of praise, prayer, and preaching. It is a time when people catch up on personal and community happenings; when formal and informal church, personal, and community business is conducted; when lost and estranged people are reunited; when relationships form and deepen; when the rest of church life is born and nourished—in short, it is in every way a family reunion. Larger churches have specialized programs to meet particular needs, but in small churches many of these diverse needs are addressed within the context of worship. In and through worship, pastoral care happens, mission happens, Christian education happens, and church maintenance happens.

In Chapter 2 I identified ten characteristic marks or qualities of small churches. If a small church were to keep them in mind when it thinks about and plans for worship, its worship would be more authentic and appropriate. The following are some of the implications of each small-church quality for small-church worship:

1. The small church is its own common expectations. Worship needs to be harmonious with the expectations people bring. If people are expecting their church to be intimate and personal but worship is formal and impersonal, they will leave with needs unmet. Changes in their worship that are consistent with their expectations will be met with openness. Knowing the expectations of the worshipers is essential to planning worship that fits. Sometimes expectations need to be challenged. If people expect mediocrity, they need help in elevating their expectations. Lazy singing, mumbled responses, sloppy preaching, and a humdrum atmosphere should be identified and rectified.

2. Almost everyone knows everyone else in small churches. That is often more myth than fact. Do the youngest know the oldest and vice versa? The newcomer may have been introduced to the regulars, but that does not mean they know each other. Those who do not know everyone but who think everyone else does will feel especially left out.

People will worship differently when almost everyone knows everyone. On the one hand, they will feel in place and at home. On the other hand, they may feel greater need to protect their privacy. They will be glad to be together but careful about being too transparent. The preacher must address the needs of the people without being so direct (with words or looks) that privacy is trespassed upon. People are willing to be more informal with people they know, but often less willing to risk themselves.

Even in very small churches, I've seen name tags worn periodically as a means of assisting the unknown or unknowing to know and be known. We've mimeographed a Church Family Album containing interesting information about each person, so that the people behind the faces can be known. When we stop knowing one another, we stop being a small church.

3. There is a sense of "family." In times of both trouble and joy, the first ones we usually call are "family." The next step beyond knowing everyone is discovering that those others care and can be counted on, like family. In small-church worship there is potential time and space for feelings and concerns to be shared, celebrated, empathized with, and reacted to. At our church these sharings during our Time of Joys and Concerns have ranged from joy at the birth of a calf, to grief over tragedy, to news about illness, to requests for help, to concerns about public issues. It has been a time for laughter, tears, and healing prayers. At one time or another, most of our members have felt free to share verbally at this point in the worship.

The sense of family has other ramifications for worship. As when the family clan gathers, there is less politeness but more concern. The business of the day—the worship service—may get sandwiched between other family business. The humor in the worhsip will be less in the form of jokes and canned stories and more in the form of "in" jokes and stories from the family memory. As in family reunions the process for the time together may be determined less by a printed order of worship than by a shared sense of the right way to proceed. Preachers will discover that family gatherings are less likely to endure long monologues than gatherings of polite strangers.

4. Everyone feels important, significant, and needed. Small-church worship is particularly suited to considerable lay participation and participation by all ages. Wise worship planners could see that in a space of three or four months everyone is asked to do something—read, sing, count, take the offering, light candles, make a banner, and so on. Specific birthdays, anniversaries, and special events can be recognized. Each week the worshiping congregation could hold up a different person or family in prayer. The small church can see that each worshiper knows Jesus meant him or her when he talked about the lost coin, sheep, and son and the pearl of great price.

5. Organizational functioning is simple. Information that is announced clearly will reach most church members. An item of church business or concern can be aired, and sometimes even resolved, during a time of announcements or sharing or after worship. In larger churches, people gather at one time to worship, at another to socialize, and at another to do business. A small-church worship gathering, like a good potluck meal, is likely to be a combination of both. It may well be a time of inspiration and acting upon the inspiration. Liturgical purists may be appalled at this union of worship and work, but those who see all God's work as holy will understand.

6. The church's identity is in its collective personality more than in its programs. Few people will join a small church for its great range of programs, since there probably is no such range. Instead, they choose it or reject it for its personality. A wise small church will follow the ancient advice "know thyself" and then tailor its worship to portray and highlight that unique self.

If the church is friendly, its worship should be warm and affectionate. If it is diverse, it should celebrate its diversity.

60

If the young are plentiful, then let the worship pulsate with youthful zest. If it is a silver-haired congregation, let it confirm its rich tradition and be thankful for each fruitful moment. If it is the church at the head of the town common or square, let its worship speak to the whole community. If it is the remnant of a once large urban church, hold up the plentiful remnant passages from the Old Testament and the New Testament stories of the fledgling Christian churches fighting for survival among the principalities and powers of the dominant Roman world. If it is a small ethnic church, let its worship affirm its own special people in this place as well as the church universal. A church's worship should be organic to its nature.

7. The membership will claim a common history and a common future. Worship can be a time for celebrating significant church milestones or the memory of some of their own important saints or the particular dreams the members are pursuing. Even churches in the "free church" tradition could revive All Saints' Day as a time of remembering. Christmas and Easter are only two of the seasons when a church might anticipate its common future.

The propensity for remembering and anticipating can be used in special services. A service celebrating a couple's golden wedding anniversary can be an occasion for honoring marriage and family. A whole service devoted to the baptism or dedication of a child can be a time for recognizing the young among us and God's intention for us all.

8. Theology, which has been defined as the way we talk about God, will be experienced in personal, relational, and historical ways. God is most clearly talked about and perceived in smaller churches in the first person—what is happening between you and me, and what happened to our ancestors. This is not the limit of God, but it is a beginning for making God real. In classical theology, two words used to describe God were "omnipotent" (all powerful) and "omnipresent" (present everywhere). Each is a helpful concept, but the omnipresence of God might be more relevant for a small church. It might prefer to sing "Love Divine, All Loves Excelling" more often than "God the Omnipotent."

The parts of worship can specifically address the relation-

61

ship between God and these people, the right here, and the right now. Preaching and the other parts of the liturgy can address specific issues in the church—for example, a baptism, a death, a conflict situation. The preacher can identify real ways God is present in the parish as well as in the larger world. Prayers can be more specific and more personal. When everyone knows everyone and the caring quotient is high, God is likely to be experienced more relationally and horizontally than vertically and impersonally.

9. Mission commitments are personal and immediate. Mission is worship at work. The work can begin in worship. Prayers of intercession are mission. The offering is mission. Worship can be mission, as well as preparation for mission. Mission is often mistakenly kept separate from worship, which emasculates worship and secularizes mission.

Our youth group bought and raised a young goat for Heifer Project. When "Snowflake Love" was ready to be part of a shipment of animals to a Caribbean island, we brought her into worship and dedicated her and committed ourselves to a greater mission involvement. We could identify with a specific goat going to provide milk and offspring to a people on an island we could find on a map. She was a bridge between a small congregation and the mammoth problem of world hunger. In small-church worship, mission needs to be symbolized, objectified, and personalized, so that sincere people can comprehend and respond.

10. The small church wants a minister who is a person, pastor, and generalist. This is no place for a "pulpit voice" or an impersonal manner. When one of our deacons says I (the minister) "am no one special," it is meant as a compliment. The person of the pastor in the pulpit is a large part of the message. What message that is will depend on how authentic and available he or she is. "A preacher who is not willing to make his understanding of his own faith and doubt, anxiety and hope, fear and joy available as a source of recognition for others can never expect to remove the many obstacles which prevent the Word of God from bearing fruit."[6] When the congregation is close enough to see the whites of your eyes, you cannot hide behind robe, rhetoric, or pedigree.

62

All this is to say that a church's worship, if it is to be authentic, must be tailored to the size and nature of the congregation. Authentic worship is a come-as-you-are party hosted by God in which a congregation comes with no pretense into the presence of the host. When a small church masquerades as something it is not, it will feel out of place at the party.

THE PLACE OF WORSHIP

The places where small churches worship are as varied as the Christian church itself. They range from living rooms to huge sanctuaries which house once large congregations. The place is very important to the people who worship there, and even to many who do not.[7]

For many it is in a real sense a sanctuary or holy place safe from a threatening secular environment. Whether it is good theology or not, many people feel God is somehow more resident there than in the world at large. For others, the cross, the Bible, the chalice, and the table or altar are powerful and holy symbols of divine presence. They may also be symbols of human presence. On a few occasions I was chided for not showing proper respect for the chancel chairs and candlesticks that were memorial gifts from an earlier era.

For many it is the place where they were married, where a son was baptized, where a daughter was confirmed, where a parent is buried, and where they have attended faithfully for decades. And it is the place where people remember who made them, who they are, where they belong, and what their ministry and mission is. It is a place of pride for many; what some have helped build or furnish, others have paid dearly to keep open. For many it is the most orderly, attractive, peaceful, and hopeful place in an otherwise drab, chaotic, futile, and stressful life. Whether it resembles a shrine, oasis, or family room, the place is important to most.

The place is also important because it can make or break the worship experience. The experience of the transcendent is not likely when the environment dulls our senses instead of awakening them, and where there are no living symbols to beckon our souls. A sense of family is difficult to achieve if people are so scattered they cannot even catch a cold from one another. Most of us would choose to eat in a restaurant that is warm, attractive, and neat, as opposed to one that is cold, dismal, and shabby. Flexibility and informality are out of reach if everything is screwed down or untouchable. Everyone will not know everyone if there is no area for moving and mingling.

The place of worship for the Warwick church has more to do with the life and vitality of this church than most people realize. We have worked for four things in our worship space.

First, a worship space must enable our definition of worship. Where we worship must be both a sanctuary where we are safe in the presence of eternal God and a meeting room where we are in relationship with one another. It is not a lecture hall or an auditorium, but a stage or arena where we actively participate. It should be a living museum where we recall our history and a laboratory where we discover our future. It should feel neither so foreign that we (or our children) don't feel at home, nor so familiar that we fail to perceive. The symbols that speak to us and for us should be fertile artifacts from our sacred history and creations of our own artisans, rather than sterile selections from a slick catalog.

Our Warwick sanctuary and meeting room is neat, warm, and communicative. Five rows of pews in a semicircle allow us to sit beside one another rather than in front of or behind others. The communion table, an offering box, the minister's stoles, and the banners were made by us. The flowers are from our gardens. The baptismal bowl was made for us. The Bible, cross, and candlesticks are memorial gifts to remind us of our own saints. When we worship we are at home.

Second, the place for our family reunion should be attractive—not opulent, but attractive. A coat of paint, a mop and bucket, a new carpet runner, vibrant banners, brighter light bulbs, plants and fresh flowers are all things that can make a difference. The sixteen ten-dollar water-damaged pews we bought and refinished made a dramatic difference in our already appealing worship space. The way a church building looks and feels can tell the story of the resident people. A drab and cluttered place may well symbolize a people with a drab and cluttered faith.

Third, the lives of people cannot be touched if they are too far away to touch. Can the atmosphere be changed so the people will choose not to be untouchable and unreachable? Will they allow the back pews to be roped off or removed? Can the pulpit be moved down to the main floor so the minister is closer to and on the same level with the people? We have had as many as one hundred in worship, yet the worship leader is not more than twenty-five feet from anyone, and no one is more than forty feet from anyone else. Snow-belt pastors frequently report how much more effective their worship is when the church retreats to the chapel or fellowship hall to save oil during the winter.

Fourth, worship space should be as versatile as possible. People may feel secure if nothing changes, but they will also stop looking and listening. We unscrewed the pews to paint the floor, and they have never been reattached. We've moved them into a round for communion and replaced them with tables and chairs for a Good Friday seder-communion and a pre-wedding celebration and feast. They've been turned one way for a wedding and another way for a drama. The banners change with the church seasons. The symbols on the communion table change to contribute to a special theme. The whole space has been decorated for Pentecost, "First Fruits," and Harvest Sundays, as well as Advent-Christmas.

Worship does not always have to be in the sanctuary or even in the building. Jesus tells us (John 4:23): "The true worshipers will worship the Father in spirit and truth," not always in a special building. Once, when we were thirty in number, we arrived on a snowy morning to discover a cold building and no fuel. With little hesitation we piled into cars and went to a member's living room for worship while Sunday school was held upstairs. That is difficult to do with two hundred.

We have an annual outdoor worship service in one of the nearby state parks. Sometimes this is on Pentecost, when the service has been accompanied by helium balloons and kites. During our anniversary year we worshiped outdoors at the site of our first church building. We've worshiped in the town hall dining room and in an upstairs Sunday school room (another heatless Sunday).

I can imagine worshiping in a factory or office building on a Labor Day Sunday when we would celebrate the work life of our people. Or on Rural Life Sunday we might worship in a pasture or a hayloft. The point is that we should capitalize on the flexibility made possible by small numbers and that the people of God can celebrate God's presence in places other than sanctuaries. After all, Paul reminds us, "Do you not know that you are God's temple and that God's Spirit dwells in you? [1 Cor. 3:16]."

We need to be thoughtful and creative with what we do with our worship space and with the possibilities of alternative spaces. That space is more important than we realize. J.A.T. Robinson has said, "The church building is a prime aid, or a prime hindrance, to the building up of the Body of Christ. . . . And the building will always win."[8]

THE PRACTICE OF WORSHIP

Small churches worship not only in many places but also in many ways. Often these ways hinder their experience of the presence of God and fail to accent the possibilities of worship in small numbers. Certainly there is no one right way, even for a specific church, to worship. A church must diligently and continuously search for the most faithful and effective ways of corporately expressing themselves in worship, recognizing God's presence and hearing God's word, and responding to that holy presence and word with integrity, appropriateness, and power.

Orders of worship vary according to a church's theological and denominational tradition, customs, and the inclinations of pastor and people. Our way of worship has evolved as people, ideas, and experience have changed. The way this church worships is neither the "right" way nor the way another church should adopt carte blanche. However, a discussion of our order of worship can illustrate how a church can begin to tailor its worship to its particular size, needs, and nature. Our order allows for predictability and variety, encourages participation by all, and sees worship as a building process rather than a static event. The skeleton of our order looks like this:

> *We Prepare*
> Prelude
> Announcements
> Call to Worship
> Hymn of Praise
> Unison Prayer of Confession or Call to Confession
> Silent Prayers of Confession
> Assurance of Grace
> Gloria Patri
>
> *We Hear*
> Ministry of Children
> Favorite Hymn [while children under age eight go to child care]
> Scripture(s)
> Sermon Hymn
> Sermon
> Anthem [this often has a different place in the order]
>
> *We Respond*
> Service of Intercessions and Prayers
>   Joys and Concerns of Our Community
>   Preparation for Prayer [an ancient litany is used]
>   Silent Prayers
>   Pastoral Prayer
>   Lord's Prayer
>   Choral Response
> Offering Back to God
>   Doxology
>   Dedication Prayer
> Hymn of Reentry
> Passing of the Peace
> Commission
> Choral Benediction
> Postlude

Within each segment of the service a variety of things have been done. Almost every Sunday there is some variation, but never is everything varied. Let's look at this order piece by piece.

Prelude. The prelude serves several purposes. It tells the greeters and kibitzers in the parlor that worship is about to begin. It masks some of the cacophony of many people moving and communicating and of children struggling against quieting. For people who have been rushing since they awakened, it is time to catch their breaths before the move into the liturgy. It begins to call people from other matters to the matter at hand.

Our regular organist and cellist often include an old gospel hymn that awakens memories and feelings. Our substitute organist is a concert pianist, and when she plays, the prelude is a mini-concert that begins to stir our spirits. Sometimes our children's choir will sing as part of the prelude, which awakens the congregation to the verve and vivacity children model. We have used this time to learn a hymn or song that is used later. The prelude is warm-up time in the best sense. It is a signal, a mood inducer, and a time to get in touch and prepare.

This might be a good time for people to move around the sanctuary greeting those who are new, those who are returning, or those whom they just need to greet. Then when they are called into God's presence they will come as brothers and sisters rather than as polite acquaintances and strangers.

Announcements. Are announcements more than a necessary evil? Are they necessary? When should they be made? Our announcement time is before the Call to Worship. Some are not happy with that placement, and we may try it at the very end of worship. But announcements may have been judged unfairly. If worship is supposed to connect us with real life, then identifying the significant happenings of God's people is legitimate and deserves a rightful place. Announcements are more appropriate in smaller churches because they are more likely to be for all rather than for special groups. Announcements that catch the people's attention and focus the work of the church might actually prepare the congregation for worship.

Call to Worship. Many ministers begin worship with a prayer of invocation. I prefer a Call to Worship involving the

68

congregation as a means of getting people on their feet, into the act of worship, acknowledging who they are and why they are present, and calling upon the One who is the focus of our worship. An important question is, Who is being called? Often it seems as if we are inviting God into our presence—as if we could keep God out. Rather, we are calling the pilgrims into God's presence.

The Call can take many forms. It can be sung. Once two of our people acted a short dramatic skit that confronted the congregation with the theme of the morning. Once a hidden alarm clock startled and called people to worship. A youth dance choir from a nearby church beautifully called us to worship by means of sacred dance. Many psalms and other scriptures are appropriate Calls (e.g., Psalms 27, 42, 95, 100, 150, and Isa. 40:28-31). The Call can be lined out, a colonial practice in which the leader speaks or sings a line of scripture or song and the people send it back with the same volume and inflection. If the Call is done responsively, the congregation can be divided by sides, male and female, young and old, blue eyes and brown eyes, and so on. Hymns can be spoken or sung and used as Calls. Church school classes, a Bible study group, or a committee can be asked to write and lead Calls that are appropriate for the specific congregation. In a very small church each worshiper could be called to worship by name.

We have a new member who teaches at a school for the deaf. In an effort to still and center ourselves, she has taught us to speak in sign language "Be still and know that I am God [Ps. 46:10]." This can precede or be part of the Call.

J. Phillip Swander, worship and preaching instructor at Hartford Seminary, insists that the Call is vital to the quality and integrity of the worship which follows. He stresses that the way we call our people to worship is at least as important as the words we use. It has the same importance as the first scene in a drama. It brings the actors on stage. In the Call or opening scene, the actors identify themselves. In both, the theme of the drama is named. If the actors in the first scene are tardy, ill-prepared, or halfhearted, the whole drama is spoiled. Rather than spoiling an hour of worship, would it not be better to stop the Call and start over if the actors are not ready? Perhaps the leader is slouching, mumbling, addressing the ceiling, looking ahead to the first hymn. If the lead actor is not serious and centered, neither will the other actors be. Marshall McLuhan taught us that "the medium is the message," and the leader lets us know whether the Call is important business or merely a meaningless ritual to be hustled through.

Hymn of Praise. Music, and specifically hymn-singing, can be either one of the weakest or the strongest aspects of small-church worship. Attitude, choice of music, and environment, rather than the quantity and quality of musicians, determine which. The Warwick church is proof that a musically weak church can grow into a relatively strong one. It happened here despite a monotone minister, a director with a beautiful voice but little training, a cooperative organist with average talent, and a poor organ.

Music is at the heart of our religious tradition.

> It was the duty of the trumpeters and singers to make themselves heard in unison in praise and thanksgiving to the Lord, and when the song was raised, with trumpets and cymbals and other musical instruments, in praise to the Lord, . . . the house of the Lord was filled with a cloud, so that the priests could not stand to minister because of the cloud; for the glory of the Lord filled the house of God [2 Chron. 5:13-14].

> Do not get drunk with wine, for that is debauchery; but be filled with the Spirit, addressing one another in psalms and hymns and spiritual songs, singing and making melody to the Lord with all your heart [Eph. 5:18-19].

Song was the voice of faith for our early Christian ancestors. It was so central to the church that Ignatius, bishop of Antioch, addressed the church at Ephesus in musical metaphor:

> Your presbytery, indeed, which deserves its name and is a credit to God, is closely tied to the bishop as the strings to a harp. Wherefore your accord and harmoni-

ous love is a hymn to Jesus Christ. Yes, one and all, you should form yourselves into a choir, so that, in perfect harmony and taking your pitch from God, you may sing in unison and with one voice to the Father through Jesus Christ.[9]

The marriage between music and the early church began to break up when the Edict of Milan (A.D. 313) banned instrumental music because there might be pagan influences which could infiltrate holy worship. In A.D. 364 the Council of Laodicea took music from the congregation and decreed that only the clergy had the right to sing during the official liturgy.[10] Over a thousand years later Martin Luther sought to end clerical control and suppression of music in worship. He wrote thirty-six hymns and encouraged congregations to respond to the word with song.

As everyone who sings in the shower, hums along with the car radio, or has a teenager knows, music is the voice of the human spirit and a powerful influence on thought and life. Music in worship is not meant to be a time filler or a change of pace. If it was not important we wouldn't devote 25 percent or more of our service to music. Music tells the story of faith, strengthens personal faith, and binds together faithful people in the pews and through the centuries. Dietrich Bonhoeffer, writing about worship in the intimate Christian community, describes the place of unison singing in the service:

> Unison singing, difficult as it is, is less of a musical than a spiritual matter. Only where everybody in the group is disposed to an attitude of worship and discipline can unison singing, even though it may lack much musically, give us the joy which is peculiar to it alone. . . . The more we sing, the more joy will we derive from it, but, above all, the more devotion and discipline and joy we put into our singing, the richer will be the blessing that will come to the whole life of the fellowship from singing together.
> It is the voice of the Church that is heard in singing together. It is not you that sings, it is the Church that is singing, and you, as a member of the Church, may share in its song. Thus all singing together that is right must serve to widen our spiritual horizon, make us see *our little company* as a member of the great

Christian Church on earth, and help us willingly and gladly to join our singing, be it feeble or good, to the song of the Church.[11]

The Hymn of Praise is the first occasion when the congregation, with one voice, can praise the One who creates, sustains, and leads them on. It should help the congregation thank God for their own lives and all life, for their spiritual tradition, and for the life in community they share. Because of its strategic location in the order it should be a familiar hymn, and one that children can enjoy and comprehend. Frequently it should be a children's song that adults can enjoy and comprehend. Tempo is particularly important in this hymn, as in all hymns. How can it be a hymn of praise if it sounds like a 78RPM record being played at 45RPM? I much prefer a few missed notes to a plodding pace.

Unison Prayer of Confession or Call to Confession. For many, "sin" is a difficult word and concept. Some people feel so miserable about their own lives that they do not want to be reminded of what they already know too well. Others have no sense of sinfulness and feel no need to confess. On the one hand, we have people who feel overwhelmed by sin but cannot understand or accept God's grace. On the other hand, there are those who take grace for granted because sin is so superficial. For this part of the service to have meaning and power, there is need for reeducation and new language.

In Paul Tillich's sermon "You Are Accepted," sin is equated with separation—separation from self, others, and God.[12] Sin is not a laundry list of infractions. It is not what I do but who I am. Who frequently does not feel personally separated from self, a jumble of feelings and impulses, hopes and fears? Who is not out of relationship with significant others? Who in the pew feels truly at one with God? If people feel little need to confess, worship will have little impact for them.

People in small congregations may find a time of confession doubly difficult. First, with the fear that in a close fellowship everyone knows my business, there may be a greater tendency to keep my need for confession even more private and repressed. Second, in a small fellowship the separation we feel from certain others in the group is more difficult and threatening. Instead of being easy and general, confession may be specific and painful. It is painful because it also involves forgiving, and that is risky. When Jesus said you should not offer your gift at the altar (worship) until you are reconciled with your brother or sister (Matt. 5:22-24), he was speaking especially about relationships in small fellowships.

Confession is one more step in our preparation for hearing with openness. Sometimes scripture is used to call to confession or as a general statement of confession. A news clipping, quotation, or community event can be used to focus the current need for confession. People might be invited to share situations where they see sin and separation. We often use a general, contemporary prayer or litany of confession as a preparation for each person's confession. There might be a particular timely confession the congregation should pray together.

People could write anonymous confessions on slips of paper to be read as a litany, with the congregation responding, "Forgive us loving Lord." One Pentecost we asked people to write a specific fear in their life on a slip of paper. These were brought to the communion table and burned in a Chinese wok while the congregation sang "Every Time I Feel the Spirit." Rey O'Day and Edward Powers offer several creative confessional ideas: People can be invited to write on their bulletins the names of people with whom they wish to make peace; or they can be provided with stationery and given time to write a note to those with whom they desire reconciliation; or in an outdoor service, that which is being confessed can be written on a rock and buried in a common hole.[18]

Our corporate confession is followed by a time of silence. This is a time for each to identify those situations and relationships that are ruptured and in need of healing and grace. It is a time for confessing and forgiving and giving to God all that hinders full participation in worship. To connect the confessors, people could be asked to pray for those next to them, that each could experience forgiveness and grace that day. Allow enough silence so confession will be taken seriously.

Assurance of Grace and Gloria Patri. Tillich defines grace as the experience of reconciliation. Forgiveness and grace are the radical promises of the Christian faith. For an Assurance I use one of the biblical promises, a hymn like "Amazing Grace," a traditional assurance, a litany, or a contemporary or spontaneous one. A volunteer might describe a real experience of grace.

The Assurance is followed by standing and singing the Gloria Patri, an ancient hymn of praise to the God who has just freely wiped clean the slate. It is never sung with enough release and exultation. In many churches everyone faces the altar or communion table during the Gloria. Believing that God does not reside on a table and is not even particularly symbolized there, I face the congregation to affirm that God is present in our midst. This celebration of God in our midst is particularly appropriate for a small congregation.

Having been called, having praised, having confessed and been forgiven, it is time to stop preparing and to start hearing the word in its various forms.

Ministry of Children. John Westerhoff stresses that adults have as much to learn from children as children do from adults and that children are integral to the worship and common life of the church.[14] The relationship of children to the church is discussed more fully in Chapter 4 of this book. One of the unique and beautiful possibilities of small churches is the way they can make children an integral part of the whole. Because our church emphasizes this, we often have one third of our congregation under the age of twelve.

A variety of things occur during our Ministry of Children. Sometimes there's a traditional children's story-sermon, and sometimes a discussion with the children and with the rest of the congregation. Sometimes the children share a song, drama, or creation from church school. On occasion a child has told the story. Other adults have told the story. (Every congregation should utilize its great storytellers, who may be better than the minister.) To illustrate the value and fun of cooperation, the whole congregation once helped keep a balloon aloft. In the fashion made popular several years ago by Art Linkletter, a different child each week could be introduced and interviewed. And we have baptisms at this time.

For this part of the worship, I have several purposes. I want children to feel at home and to know they are important to us, and I want the adults to get to know and love our children. It is a time to educate children, and adults, to faith, ancestors, beliefs, and ways of church and Christian life. It is a light time, when we really are a family of faith who can laugh easily or share deeply. Most important, it is the time when we can best help children know how it felt when Jesus brushed off the disciples and called the children to him, held them, and made them his own. It is a time when we hear God's word for children *and* from children.

Favorite Hymn. People have favorite hymns that I might not choose. A time for a favorite hymn facilitates the passage of young children to Child Care as well as offering another place for lay people to have input into the service. Children often compete with adults to get their hymn chosen. And we have added some new hymns to our repertoire when we discovered one person's favorite.

Scripture. The scripture reading is always related to the rest of the service. It may or may not be from the lectionary. The scripture is presented in various ways. Since many biblical passages are written as drama or dialogue, I sometimes ask people to read the parts as a drama. Sometimes the congregation will use the pew Bibles to read the scripture in unison or responsively. On occasion it has been acted out. I often lead a short Bible study or discussion on the passage, a method that is particularly suited to a small church. This is one of several times in worship when children, youth, and adults can lead. But whoever reads must practice and rehearse to ensure that the Word is not lost, garbled, or taken lightly.

Thanks to television and the movies, we have a visual

culture. Just because scripture is read does not mean it is heard. Frequently this is the time in worship when minds wander furthest, and methods must be found to enliven the life-giving words on the page. A small congregation increases the ways the word can be heard.

Sermon Hymn. The Sermon Hymn is a bridge from the written word to the spoken words that can communicate God's word for this time and people. If we are honest, this hymn is also a time when people can move, cough, stretch. But if the hymn is well chosen and well sung it can help people open themselves to a theme, to themselves, and to God moving in them.

Sermon. In 1857 Anthony Trollope wrote, "There is perhaps no greater hardship at present inflicted on mankind in civilized and free countries than the necessity of listening to sermons."[15] Perhaps there is also no greater hardship faced by preachers than preaching in small churches. How can that be? There is the danger of not taking the preaching task seriously because there are "only" forty people out there. And the small-church preacher feels more vulnerable because he or she is so close to the congregation. Or if the whole congregation is in the back row, as happened to a lay preacher friend of mine, the gap may appear unbridgeable. And in a small church you can see who fell asleep, who's frowning, who's turned off. Because you know your people so well, you know where they are tender, opinionated, or pained, and so, desiring to protect them or yourself, you run the risk of being so vague you are innocuous. They know you so well that they know when you are ill prepared or being phony. If you are working at more than one job, there frequently is not enough time to prepare the kind of sermon even a few people deserve and need. If you are preaching to more than one congregation, it is difficult to have a sermon that is on target for both.

In preaching the preacher's depth or shallowness of faith is most clearly revealed. Preachers often mask lack of substance with slickness, substitute impotent words for a potent Word, exchange catchy stories for the real Story, and hide specific Truth behind glib generalities. Members of small churches who know the preacher well and are close enough to read her or him clearly can tell if they are being fed manna or junk food. A church that receives manna may remain small, but it will be healthy, well nourished, and nourishing to others.

Henri Nouwen suggests that there are two essential aspects of preaching—dialogue and availability.[16] Both are particularly relevant for preachers in small churches. By dialogue he means it is the task of the preacher to preach to people in terms that they can respond to with their own life experience. On occasion I have looked around our congregation before worship and was able to identify what was important in *each* person's life at that point. When you are this familiar with your people, you can address them so they get the message they need. A preacher can know only a limited number of people this well.

Second, the preacher must be personally available to the listener. In small churches where people and preacher know each other well, they can collude to avoid the issues and feelings that really matter; they can agree to keep their relationship safe and superficial. *Or* they can contract to be genuine and available to one another. With the latter kind of contract, the preacher is free to bring God's word to bear upon life as preacher and people really live it.

> If the preacher does not want to increase the resistance against the Word but decrease it, he has to be willing to lay himself down and make his own suffering and his own hope available to others so that they too can find their own, often difficult way. . . .
> Every time real preaching occurs the crucifixion is realized again.[17]

If the numerically small church is really a small church in which people know and care for one another, this kind of preaching is possible because each side of the relationship trusts the other. In small churches, where there is the greatest opportunity to be available, the preacher must decide whether to keep a stiff upper lip and put up a good front, or whether to be who he or she really is, warts and all.

Preaching in a small church is different. A sensitive

person will talk differently to forty than to two hundred. There should be more personal contact. There can even be verbal response and interaction at sermon time. When there are only a handful of births, baptisms, weddings, and deaths a year, the preacher can specifically and personally address the feelings that are part of them. When I found out after midnight one Saturday night that a young father of four and husband of our church school superintendent had been killed in a motorcycle accident, I had to prepare a new sermon so that I could address what the people were feeling. Small-church sermons tend to be more pastoral than prophetic, but the latter type is also necessary.

Since there is generally less of a public image to maintain in a small church, there tends to be more tolerance of the untraditional. I have developed an effective sermon alternative for my church—a one-person, Hal Holbrook / Mark Twain style of dramatization. I have costumed and been Peter twice, one of the disciples on the road to Emmaus, and Johnny Appleseed. These "sermons" have received the most positive response of any I preached. Occasionally I have used a film for part or all of the sermon. Gradually more and more of our lay people are accepting the invitation to talk about their faith and life from the pulpit. The small church is the right size for real interpersonal communication—which is what preaching ought to facilitate.

Anthem. Our anthem usually follows the sermon, but not always. It can be used wherever it fits—as a call to worship, as a prayer, as an assurance of grace, or even as a part of the sermon. What it should not be is a performance, a filler to avoid silence, or something the congregation can do as well. If the choir is just singing out of the hymnbook, why not let the congregation join in? It is the choir's job to express, amplify, or elevate the theme or feeling that is appropriate for that point of worship. When worship is well planned and well acted, the choir will sing what the congregation is feeling.

One beauty of music in small churches is the informality and naturalness that is possible. In my first weeks at the

Warwick church the choir took off their robes and became part of the congregation. Frequently a choir member will be singing with a child in arms. While our choir members may not be even semi-professional, they sing well what they sing and they express well what we feel.

Service of Intercessions and Prayers. Following the speaking and the singing of the word, it is time for the congregation to respond—by praying and giving. A small church can do this especially meaningfully. We begin this period with a time of sharing. Two extremes of what happens were illustrated by one of our high school students. One spring her family's few cows were being very prolific. On several Sundays she joyfully announced the birth of a new calf. And on another Sunday she sobbed as she shared her concern for a seriously ill aunt. The congregation wrapped her in their care and the aunt in their prayers. Our sharing time is used for everything from personal thanks, joys, concerns, needs, and sorrows, to concern about town and world issues.

The Pastoral Prayer is preceded by a time of silent prayer. Our people appreciate silence and are asking for more. My prayers are usually spontaneous as I try to raise up the themes of the hour, the feelings of the moment, and the concerns that have been shared. On occasion the congregation will participate verbally in the prayer, or through a bidding prayer, when I will suggest subjects and they will pray silently. Once or twice a year the congregation will write prayers of thanksgiving or concern, and these will be submitted and read by the leader. This congregation is becoming a praying church.

Offering Back to God. This is another way of involving the congregation. Each Sunday we have different ushers, men and women, children and adults, newcomers and old-timers. What they lack in smoothness they make up for in sincerity. We are working to transform the offering from the time people reach in to pay the bills to a time when we reach out and commit ourselves and our resources to a life of stewardship, of taking care of our sector of the universe. Now we bring *all* the money to the communion table—the church school offering, the proceeds from the fair, auction, dinners, and so forth—to be used in our common ministry and mission. Instead of having ushers come to them, the people could be asked to bring their offerings to the altar. On a special Sunday they could be asked to offer a symbol from their daily life (e.g., a school book, hammer, calculator, or cookbook) to symbolize their daily ministry.

Hymn of Reentry. The principal reason for coming to worship is to be outfitted for a life of discipleship outside. Our ending hymn, which is also a beginning hymn, should get us on our feet and prepared to move outward. It is not the time for a new hymn (unless they learned it before worship). It should be an action hymn that communicates what you want people to do. This is not the time for people to be stuffing things back in their purses and pockets.

Passing of the Peace. This is an ancient Christian custom. The greeting in 1 Peter 5:14 is a typical New Testament church greeting: "Greet one another with the kiss of love. Peace to all of you that are in Christ." I have seen churches where the Peace was passed reluctantly as if leprosy was feared. Members of small churches, like most families, generally are not afraid to touch. Each worshiper gets a greeting and a handshake or hug. Sometimes the greeting is changed to make it more appropriate. On our "Apple Sunday" Johnny Appleseed passed out apples to all, along with the greeting "You are the apple of God's eye" (see Deut. 32:10).

Commission. Instead of a passive benediction we have an active commission, when the worshipers are sent out to perform their own ministries. This is similar to the commissioning of a ship when, after building is complete, a champagne bottle is smashed against the hull and the vessel slides into the water for a life of service outside the harbor.

Our basic order of worship, just outlined, is orderly, flexible, involving, and evolving. It is a good order because it maximizes what is good and possible for a small number of worshipers. It encourages participation, intimacy, and response. It includes both the young and the new and affirms all.

Like all churches, small churches worship on sacramental occasions and at festive and seasonal times. Like families, small churches look forward to and enjoy gathering for special and traditional events and celebrations.

Baptism. Theologically, we enter the church by baptism. The word christening came from the time when it was the church who conferred on an infant the "Christian" name. Baptism is a sign and seal of our inclusion in God's family and the family of faith. When children or infants are baptized, it is a promise by the child's family and the church family to take responsibility for loving the child and nurturing him or her in the faith. Only a small church can make this a personal and genuine promise as a whole church. One thing a small church can do expertly is care for small people, and for this reason baptism is and should be a big occasion in small churches.

Before we baptize one of our own, I invite the congregation to bring a card or letter for the child, offering a prayer, hope, dream, or vision that can be shared later with the child. The whole congregation stands in a tight circle around the family, deacons, and me at the entrance to our sanctuary. The child could be taken to each person for a blessing or greeting. Baptism can also be a time to give special recognition to all the children. And it should always be within the context of corporate worship, since it is the church family who baptize and not the minister.

The Lord's Supper. Another sacramental time when we worship is the monthly gathering around the Lord's table. Another thing small churches enjoy is eating together. Families and people who care about one another eat together. Even potluck suppers might be seen as sacraments without religious words. New Testament churches regularly gathered in homes, ate together, and shared the Lord's

Supper. This was done in remembrance of Jesus Christ and as a celebration of their life together now and forever in Christ.

It is around the Lord's table that the small church might best discover and experience its essence and possibility. Was it merely accidental that the Lord's Supper we commemorate originally was an intimate (though quarrelsome) supper for the twelve apostles rather than a banquet for a crowd? Bonhoeffer concludes his *Life Together* by expressing what is supposed to happen around the table:

> The fellowship of the Lord's Supper is the superlative fulfillment of Christian fellowship. . . . Here joy in Christ and his community is complete. The life of Christians together under the Word has reached its perfection in the sacrament.[18]

A small church can truly, even physically, gather around the table. Our table is a simple, Shaker-style cherry table carefully crafted by Clyde, one of our young men. We use homemade bread baked by our church bakers. Our organist often contributes some of her homemade fermented grape juice. I especially remember when one of our women spontaneously began singing "Let Us Break Bread Together" as the elements were passed, and we all joined in. We traditionally end our communion service by taking hands and forming a family circle around our sanctuary, singing a benediction and passing the Peace.

There was considerable discussion concerning what age our children should be before they are served communion. After careful thought and a change of our collective minds, we have concluded that the whole family of God should be welcome at the table. Would we refuse to feed a new member of our biological family? A child we have welcomed to the family through baptism is no longer turned away from the family table.

Marriage and death ceremonies. Consistent with the image of worship as a family reunion, weddings and funerals are the other times family clans come together. When the bride, groom, or deceased is a part of the church family, this family should gather to honor, celebrate, support, grieve, and remember. I would like to see our weddings, funerals, and memorial services be like our other worship experiences, with an emphasis on congregational participation. Funerals should be planned so that they are not morbid and frightening to children (and adults). The leave-taking of a loved one should be a good and healthy experience for whole families. Funerals need not be adults only occasions.

Church year. Families come together to celebrate festive occasions and so does the church. Advent has become a special time here. At the Advent Workshop we make personal and church preparations for Christmas. At this time our worship has more of a family and intergenerational emphasis. Christmas Eve is a marvelous and mysterious time when the chapel is filled for a candlelight cantata and communion service.

Lent and Easter are just as important to small churches as they are to larger ones. One memorable Holy Week experience was a catacomb worship reenactment, when we gathered in our candlelit church basement, sat on the floor, and shared homemade soup and bread. We sang and recited scripture from memory, shared faith testimonies, and passed the bread and juice to our brothers and sisters in Christ. It was not difficult to imagine ourselves back some nineteen hundred years to a gathering of a small early church in a remote catacomb. Two days later we gathered in our town cemetery to welcome the sun and the risen Christ.

Use any excuse to assemble the church family for a special reunion or celebration. Let traditions develop around such occasions as graduations, Children's Day, and homecoming. In addition to Pentecost and Thanksgiving, we have commemorated Heritage Sunday, Family Life Sunday, Rural Life Sunday, Reformation Day, First Fruits Sunday, Harvest Sunday, and Old Home Day.

PLANNING FOR CHANGE IN WORSHIP

In the belief that worship is where the small church starts, any attempts to revive or change a small church should begin with worship. In the "great awakening" of our church, we started with worship and our Sunday morning time together. A weekly coffee hour, an emphasis on families and children, a more informal and participatory order of worship, and more frequent communion were all introduced in our first months. Each of these alterations changed the nature and quality of our worship. And, as with a pebble in a pond, each contributed to other developments in the life of our church. One of the advantages of life in a small church is that the ripple effect reaches everyone. With a simple organizational structure and fewer people to reach, the effects of a change in worship can quickly be felt in other aspects of the church's life.

If a group of people in a church want their worship to have more vitality and impact, they might use the following five-step process:

1. Have a representative group of people come together and wrestle with these questions:

- What is the unique personality of our church?
- What are our visions or hopes for our church?
- What do we each want/need from worship?
- How does our present order of worship reflect or not reflect who we are and what we believe?
- What about the present service are we indifferent to or unhappy with?
- What do we feel good about and want to see expanded or amplified?

2. Ask, what could we do differently when we come to worship that would better express who we are, reflect what we believe, and move us toward what we want? Let the ideas flow freely and list them all. At this point do not be constrained by the realities as you perceive them.

3. Then look closely at the list of ideas and decide which changes are feasible, which would be most likely to be accepted, which would be most likely to succeed, which would be most likely to breed interest and enthusiasm, and which is most important. Start with the ones that are most acceptable and most promising.

4. Make, and review, one or two changes at a time. Involve

as many people as possible in a change. Implement ideas and changes with advance, clear, and complete explanations. Give assurance that constructive feedback is desired and that the innovations will be reviewed after a fair trial.

5. After the fair trial, make alterations and proceed. There are three primary review questions:

- Has the change made our worship and time together more valuable and productive for most of us?
- Has the change moved our larger vision any closer to reality?
- What modifications in the idea would make it more palatable and profitable for our people and more effective in the realization of our vision?

When considering or planning for change, particularly in the worship life of the church, there are a variety of considerations to keep in mind:

- Find out which symbols, places, and practices in the church are sacred, and to how many and whom, and for what reasons.
- Start with sure successes—changes that will feel good to almost everyone.
- Do not initiate change all by yourself. Have some solid support behind you, or give solid support to others who are initiating the change. (Probably if only one or only a few want the change it is not a legitimate or timely one for the church.)
- Make changes for a purpose, not for the sake of change.
- Let the children lead. The children's choir can sing the new song you want the congregation to sing in three weeks. If there is reluctance about too much informality, begin by confining the informality to the "children's sermon."
- Set time limits for the experiment.
- Help people develop an attitude of tolerance, so each person does not expect that every action will suit him or her.
- For every change that is made, spotlight and affirm other traditional practices that are not being changed.

Also, some liturgical practices that might be adopted (e.g., the kiss of peace, lining out scripture and hymns, sacred dance, and spontaneous verbal prayers by the congregation) are reclaimed very old traditions. Make sure people know that.

- Love the sheep as you lead them to new pastures. "Congregations, particularly small congregations, have a way of becoming enthusiastic about whatever their pastor is enthusiastic about (if they are certain that the pastor is *their* pastor)."[19]

Worship is one thing for which small churches are the right size. If its worship has life and integrity, the church will have life and integrity. The Call to Worship used on a Sunday when we celebrated small churches, captures the place of worship in small churches:

L: Come, worship God who creates all things, large and small.
P: Let us worship Creator God.
L: Come, worship God who loves all churches, large and small.
P: Let us worship our loving God.
L: Come, let us celebrate the small church and its important place in God's Good Plan.
P: Let us celebrate and renew ourselves for our important work as one of God's small and mighty churches.

FOR DISCUSSION

1. How is your worship a "family reunion," or is it mostly an adults-only occasion?

2. In your church is worship the "work of the people," or are the people mostly spectators? Which way do you want it?

3. Does your place of worship enhance or handicap what you want to have happen in worship? What changes are feasible, desirable?

4. If your worship were really to reflect the uniqueness of your church and its opportunities, what would it be like?

CHAPTER 4

education: can anything good grow in nazareth?

Early in Jesus' ministry, Philip was telling Nathanael about Jesus. He said, "We have found him of whom Moses in the law and also the prophets wrote, Jesus of Nazareth, the son of Joseph." Nathanael responded: "Can anything good come out of Nazareth? [John 1:45-46]." The small rural town of Nazareth was so insignificant that people scoffed at the notion that someone significant might come from there. /

When we recall the boy Jesus, who amazed the elders in the Jerusalem temple, and the man Jesus, who amazed everyone twenty years later, it appears that there was an effective religious education program at the Nazareth synagogue. It would have been the rabbi and perhaps the elders of the local synagogue who helped Jesus learn both the letter and the spirit of the Jewish law and scriptures and helped shape the mind and character of the Jesus we worship and follow.

Like many of our religious education programs today, Jesus' sabbath school probably offered:

- Attention to the person, needs, and potential of each learner, so that what was within could be nourished and fulfilled, and the person might "grow in wisdom and stature"
- A transmission of the Hebrew heritage as the learner's

own story, so that the person might discover roots, identity, and a sense of being "in favor with God"

- And a place in the family of faith that gave learners a place where they belonged and were at home and in favor with all people

In short, the Nazareth synagogue education program, along with Jesus' family, apparently helped Jesus learn who and whose he was and what he was to be about. The small-church education program is similarly uniquely capable of offering its few learners personal attention, a personal heritage, and a personal place and identity in the family of faith.

Our Warwick church school has approximately fifty infants through adults in six classes. The schoolrooms are not decorated or furnished as nicely as catalog pictures. The teachers are not as well trained or prepared as I wish they were. We cannot afford the resources and equipment that are taken for granted elsewhere. We do not have the number of learners that communicates success in our world. Yet we have a faithful and effective church school and education program that helps persons learn and accept who and whose they are and what they are to be about. And that is the basic task of Christian education.

Our four-year-old daughter, Noel, asked her mother one Saturday, in the middle of a game, "Mama, is tomorrow Sunday?" After being told yes, she exclaimed, "O neat!" A six-year-old, Sarah, queried her mother, "All the people at church are part of *our* family, aren't they?" And after the birth of a baby sister, Sarah had the following conversation with her mother:

Sarah: Is Baby Beth God's daughter?
Mother: Yes, she is.
Sarah: Is Joshua [her brother] God's son?
Mother: Yes, he is.
Sarah: And I'm God's daughter, aren't I?
Mother: Yes, Sarah, you are.
Sarah: Then Daddy must be God's brother!

Eight-year-old Chuck, on a questionnaire passed out to adults, volunteered to be the church school superintendent.

And at our Good Friday catacomb service he confessed to the forty children, youth, and adults: "In the few years that I've been at the church, I've learned that God is my power." Janet, a woman in her forties, identifies two recent church learning experiences as being life-transforming for her.

As illustrated by Noel, our children feel at home at church. As illustrated by Sarah, they identify themselves as part of our church family and God's family. As illustrated by Chuck, they know that the church school is theirs and that there are important things to be learned at church. As illustrated by Janet, growing in wisdom and stature is not just "kid's stuff" here.

Christian education is not "kid's stuff." Rather, it is a basic task of the Christian church. It is as essential to the present and future of the church as secular education is to the present and future of society and culture. In fact, it is needed to ferment persons who will be yeast in the larger society and culture. Those of us in small churches or small educational programs must give careful attention to Jesus' commission to make disciples, baptize them, and help them learn all the teachings and commandments of our religious tradition.

When catalogs, curriculum, and seminary offerings are perused, one sometimes gets the impression that the typical church Christian education program is financed by an affluent, sophisticated church, housed in a many-roomed and well-equipped building, staffed by a large, trained team of enablers, and populated by many students who are led through a comprehensive learning program. Such an education program does not happen often.

If a majority of our American churches are small (under two hundred members), probably close to three-quarters of our church schools are small (seventy-five members or less). For example, United Methodist statistics for 1978 indicate that 73.8 percent of their churches have seventy-four or fewer students in attendance in their church schools.[1] There are many New England Churches of three hundred to five hundred members which have church schools of thirty to fifty.

This chapter discusses what is possible in the smaller Christian education program. It is founded on the assumptions that these small ventures in faith development can be faithful and effective and that, because of their small size, they have a unique opportunity to grow Christian persons. I offer a theology and philosophy for a small education program, a description of the unique opportunities as well as problems present in this setting, and some ideas and options appropriate for small learning situations.

A "SMALL" THEOLOGY AND PHILOSOPHY
OF EDUCATION

If you wanted to grow a healthy, loving Christian person, what kind of environment or growing medium would you choose? I would choose one with these characteristics:

- A place that is inviting, where people feel at home and part of the whole, not overwhelmed or depersonalized
- A situation that provides individual attention and recognition and attends to individual needs and potentials
- A special community or family of people that is accepting, loving, and nurturing
- An atmosphere where there are ideas, issues, feelings, and experiences that engage, challenge, stimulate, and nourish
- A presentation and experience of the Christian faith, tradition, and church that encourage rootage, identity, and commitment
- An opportunity to apply and practice the learnings that lead to a Christian style of life

This kind of environment or growing medium can be found in churches of all sizes and shapes, but it is particularly organic and natural in a small church or education program. What small churches can do naturally, larger churches often have to do synthetically—by dividing into smaller units or creating special situations (e.g., retreats, interest centers, study or task groups).

The small church is uniquely suited to adopt people into the Christian family and to nurture them in the faith. Yet until recently the educational ministry of the small church was maligned, taken for granted, or ignored. John Westerhoff confesses to having been part of this attitude:

> Recently, I discovered the large, important world of the small church. As a professional church educator, I had often ignored these thousands of small churches and, like other church educators, I had gotten used to talking about educational plants, supplies, equipment, curriculum, teacher training, age-graded classes, and learning centers with individualized instruction. Lately, I've been confronted by churches which share a pastor and will probably never be able to afford the services of a professional church educator. At best they have a couple of small inadequate rooms attached to their church building, no audiovisual equipment, few supplies, an inadequate number of prospective teachers, and not enough students for age-graded classes. . . . Most small churches will never be able to mount up or support the sort of schooling and instruction upon which religious education has been founded since the turn of the century.[2]

Perhaps some small-church educational programs could be considered sick and failures. Perhaps many biblically illiterate, morally insensitive, and ecclesiastically apathetic people stumble or stalk out of our small churches. However, even when the teachers are poorly suited, trained, and prepared, when the classroom resembles the back corner of a garage sale, when the curriculum is stale or offensive, and when there are not enough students (even for a good game of Bible baseball), many healthy, whole, and holy persons emerge.

After admitting that he had once ignored the small-church Sunday school, consigning it to the educational infirmary, John Westerhoff writes that he has come to see the old-fashioned Sunday school, which was small and personal, as the prototype for Christian education as it should be. In recalling the old Sunday school movement, Westerhoff cites a 1905 address by John Vincent entitled "A Forward Look for the Sunday School," delivered before the Eleventh International Sunday School Convention in Toronto.

[Vincent] began with an important observation, namely, that it is possible to make too much of method, of recent educational theory, of curricula, teaching, and intellectual training. . . . Then Vincent made a prediction: In the future the Sunday school will be less like a school and more like a home. Its program will focus on conversation and the interaction of people rather than the academic study of the Bible or theology. The Sunday school will be a place where friends deeply concerned about Christian faith will gather to share life together.[3]

After recalling the contributions of others of the Sunday school movement, John Westerhoff summarizes:

The old Sunday school appears to have cared most about creating an environment where people could be Christian together and where persons could experience Christian faith and see it witnessed to in the lives of significant people. The old Sunday school seemed to be aware of the importance of affections, of storytelling, of experience, of community sharing, and of role models. While many of these remain in the rhetoric of the modern church school movement, we seem to have created an institution more concerned with teaching strategies, instructional gimmicks, and curricular resources than with spiritual mentors; more concerned with age-graded classes for cognitive growth than with communities concerned with the affections; more concerned with the goals of knowing about the Bible, theology, and church history than with communities sharing, experiencing, and acting together in faith.[4]

While the small church may not be proficient at turning out biblical scholars and theological sophisticates, it is well suited to "enculturate" persons into the family and life of faith. There are three reasons for this.

First, *each person is* (or can be) *known* in the small church. When the church baptizes someone into the faith, it acknowledges that person's Christian name. When we baptize a child, we sing (to the tune of BUNESSAN, often used with "Morning Has Broken"):

[Name], we name you: And with thanksgiving
offer our prayers and sing you this song.
We are the church: your spiritual family.
Sing we our praises to Christ the Lord.

In a small church each individual—including each child —can be known by name and as a unique and special person by the whole church family. The first step in the life of faith is to be known by name. God called Abram, Abraham and made him father of a nation. At Jesus' baptism, Jesus was claimed and identified by God with the words "You are my own dear Son. I am well pleased with you [Mark 1:11, TEV]." Then his ministry could begin. Jesus chose Simon, named him Peter, and called him to a life of discipleship. God called Saul, Paul, and his life was dramatically transformed.

When someone is hospitalized, the whole church can and often does respond personally. When a student gets an award at school, the whole church is proud and communicates it. When someone appears after a long absence, you never know who will meet the returning person with a hug and a warm "We missed you!" Each person is known not only by those in his or her class, generation, group, or pew, but by the *whole* church as it worships, works, and plays. The small church incarnates the parables of the lost sheep, coin, and son with its identification and concern for the individual.

Each person's needs and gifts can be recognized and addressed. Our daughter had meningitis as a toddler and lost two-thirds of her hearing, but never is she ignored at church because people have to repeat or speak up. Never has she been ridiculed by other children because she sometimes mishears. Instead, her church accepts and loves her. A major part of what she has learned here is that this is how Christian people care for one another.

In the same way, individual gifts can be identified, developed, and celebrated. As part of our Easter worship, eight-year-old Michael played a brass duet with his uncle. This was a week after he had stuffed two hundred Easter letter envelopes, and soon after he sat in on a Ways and Means Committee meeting with his parents and told the schoolbus driver the next day everything "our" church was planning. Michael knew he was an integral part of the church.

God may know the number of hairs on each of our heads, but people do not have that ability. We can only know well a limited number of people. Particularly in a small-town small church, all of each person can be known—family situation, school performance, leisure interests, community involvements, personal needs. True, many may know your business, but that can be more helpful than harmful. Only by knowing the whole person can we minister to the whole person.

Second, the small church is uniquely suited to initiate persons into the faith because *each person is needed and does make a difference.* It is common for children and youth, not to mention adults, to feel that they don't count, that no one notices them or needs them. But in a small church, children are seen *and* heard, and each child can be included and given responsibility. The gifts that can be identified because each person is known can and should be utilized because each is needed. In our church we work to see that almost everyone has a role. Children help take the offering in worship, and their church school offering is brought to the communion table with the other offerings. The gifts of children and youth, as well as adults, can be utilized in all areas of the church—mission, worship, evangelism, caring, and maintenance, as well as education. And participation and responsibility in each area is Christian education.

Barbara, a retired woman who moved to Warwick about four years ago, summarizes this for all of us: "I feel people here make me feel needed. There are useful things I can do that in a big church I didn't get a chance to do. I feel it's the place I should have been all my life." Barbara's involvement here has been a significant part of her Christian education.

A jargon word in the church has been "empowerment," which is the belief that the gospel empowers people to control their own lives and to touch the lives of others. In the small church where each person is a big fish in a small pond, empowerment is a fact of life. People of all ages discover that they really do make a difference and are key pieces in the church-family mosaic. Ephesians 4:16, TEV, reads: "So when each separate part works as it should, the whole body grows and builds itself up through love." In the small church each separate part can have a job and have it integrated with the whole body.

Third, the small church is uniquely suited to assimilate people because *each person is part of a family of faith*

94

network. Children and youth will never learn to identify in any important way with Moses, Jeremiah, Jesus, and Paul if they cannot first identify with the saints, the pillars, and the characters in their own church family. In small churches there is an interaction and often an intimacy among persons and generations who are related not by blood but by faith affiliation. Marion Copeland, our grand lady with the great hats, will not be forgotten by the many Sunday school children she taught over several decades. And during our 150th anniversary year it was very important for our children to hear all the stories of our church history from Charlie Morse, our venerable town and church historian.

The close proximity of the old with the young helps the young know not only that they are God's (which is difficult to grasp) but also that they are the church's (which they can grasp). And the close proximity of the young with the old helps the old know they have not preserved the church in vain. One of our older saints recalls the struggle to keep our church open through many difficult years because it was important that there be a Sunday school in Warwick. Perhaps our Sunday school saved our church.

It is delightful to watch the pleasure in the faces of our retirees when our children's choir sings or when some children share in worship, and to watch grandmothers holding other people's babies and toddlers during worship. Our adults seem to enjoy our children more than the children's story during our Ministry of Children. A beautiful, unplanned ritual has developed in our church. Rotha is responsible for the flowers that grace the sanctuary from April to November. Each Sunday after worship the small children flock around her, and she prepares a special bouquet for each. Rotha makes the young feel special, and they in turn help her feel needed. In the small-church family, the old give the young a history and tradition, the young give the old a hope and a future, and each generation gives special meaning to the other.

As the small church plans its educational ministry, it needs to remember the special gifts it has: (1) Each person is known; (2) each person is needed and makes a difference; and (3) each person is part of a family of faith network. If each of these attributes is recognized and built upon as the small church designs and implements its education ministry, that ministry will be both faithful and effective, regardless of whether there be five students or seventy-five.

It is essential to have a basic and agreed-upon understanding of the what and why of Christian education. But that has little value unless a church follows through and makes the when, where, who, and how of growing Christian people consistent with its what and why.

WHEN DOES EDUCATION HAPPEN?

Christian education occurs in both formal and informal settings. Formal settings are intentional, specific situations and programs—Sunday school, confirmation and membership classes, study groups, camps, conferences, retreats, youth groups, and so on. In smaller churches there will usually be fewer of these formal times of education because of limited numbers of members, including leaders.

But there are other learnings going on throughout the church that we are probably overlooking.

> In addition to the planned education experiences, we need to be aware that many kinds of unplanned teaching/learning occur. Doors too heavy and seats too high can teach little children that church is meant for grown-ups rather than for children. Steep steps and dark hallways may teach that the church is not meant for the lame or the elderly. Bickering between groups or individuals, or financial decisions that put concern for non-essentials in the local church ahead of sharing beyond the local church, may teach persons that the church *says* one thing but does another. In evaluating Christian education in terms of the whole person, therefore, we need to consider the unplanned learnings that are constantly occurring along with the planned teaching experiences.[5]

Education is happening all the time! What is being learned informally in your church when each person is in the building, participating in worship, serving on a committee, being in a group, going to Sunday school, or attending a special event? Does the informal learning support or contradict the teaching and learning that occurs in your formal education programs? Perhaps the Christian education committee should talk with the trustees or building committee about what the building is teaching people, and with the deacons, vestry, pastor, and so on, about what the atmosphere before, during, and after worship and meetings is teaching. Perhaps it would be beneficial to do something as unusual as having those responsible for the building crawl around the building on their hands and knees for fifteen minutes to see what it looks and feels like from another perspective—the perspective of our younger children.

Youth ministry occurs when young people are being helped to find their place in church and society. Churches traditionally do this with church school classes, membership or confirmation programs, and youth groups. Peer groups are particularly important for adolescents and small churches should probably provide them if the available youth are interested and a caring adult is willing to help.

Small churches can also carry on a viable youth ministry by helping youth find and perform their own ministry in and out of the church. There is no legitimate task of the church that young people are too young to assume, and small churches are the right size to guarantee they have the opportunity. The youth Jeremiah protested that he was too young to speak for God and God responded, "Do not say, 'I am only a youth'; for to all to whom I send you you shall go . . . [Jer. 1:6-7]."

How about the time of formal Christian education? The prevalent pattern in New England is during the worship hour. While this solves the "What can we do with the children during worship" question and is convenient for parents, it is a highly questionable practice in terms of its implications. It means teachers cannot worship. If worship really is crucial for building and sustaining faith, then teachers, who are the faith guides of children and youth, need to worship more than anyone. In many small churches teenagers are part of the teaching staff. This can be a marvelous experience for them, but they as much as anyone need to be part of worship. And some of the best teaching prospects will refuse to teach if they have to miss worship. The result is that you often end up with teachers who love kids (great!) but who have little spiritual sensitivity and faith commitment (help!). Also, having worship and education simultaneously communicates that adults already "know it all" and do not need to learn, and that worship is an activity for adults only. But worship thoughtfully conceived can be meaningful for all ages.

And having worship and education at the same time often excludes the only person in the church with formal training in Christian education—the minister—from direct participation in the education of the young. This is analogous to forbidding the player-manager of the baseball team to watch, play, or coach the game. Finally, when the young are sent upstairs, downstairs, or out back, the family-of-faith network is being broken up rather than built up. Nowhere in the Gospels is there a record of Jesus sending the children off to play, or even to sabbath school, while he talked with the adults.

Church school held on another day besides Sunday solves some problems but usually creates others. After trying various models, our preference is the tradition many churches still use or have returned to. We have an education hour for everyone prior to worship and have all but our youngest children in worship for the whole service. (We provide child care for children under age eight.) Some advantages of this method are:

- Adults can reconsider the importance of education for themselves.
- Teachers feed their own faith and maintain their own relationships in the family of faith.
- Children learn the art and importance of worship.
- Worship planners and leaders are obliged to keep the words, actions, and process of worship short, comprehensible, and dramatic—a favor to children *and* adults.
- The vivacity of the children can become contagious and transforming for the whole worship atmosphere.

- Coordination between what happens in each hour is possible. (The worship hour can incorporate the themes, art, music, prayers, and litanies from the education hour.)

WHERE DOES EDUCATION HAPPEN?

Where does education happen in the church? Everywhere. When the women's group meets—whether to study the Bible, wrap bandages, or plan the next fair—the potential for real Christian education is present. When the deacons meet they can simply rehearse how to distribute communion smoothly, or they can think theologically about who is welcome at the Lord's table. The mission committee might roll up its sleeves and go to work on how to raise the money for a pet mission project, or it could first spend three meetings in Bible study, theological reflection, and analysis of world needs and issues in order to understand better the imperatives for Christian mission today. And if the education committee sees its job as more than recruiting teachers and locating curriculum that will keep children, teachers, and parents happy, it could seriously consider why and how one comes to and grows in the Christian faith. The whole church is a setting for Christian education, and each component of the church would do well to examine how it contributes to or detracts from the growth of Christian people and Christian community. Each of our own planning and program groups has found it exciting and valuable to spend time wrestling with the basic questions as the first part of their task.

Physical setting is important for education. Studies have shown that it is more difficult to stimulate people when the environment is not stimulating. It does not take much money to provide an attractive, comfortable environment for the sharing of the "greatest story ever told." What it does take is a little thought, ingenuity, scavenging and recycling, time, and some elbow grease.

One early memorable event occurred when our teachers recognized how drab our learning environment was. A gallon of brick-red floor paint, a gallon of bright yellow wall paint, a quart of white enamel, and a quart of lime-green enamel were purchased with money squeezed from our tiny treasury. One evening a dozen workers painted ceiling, walls, woodwork, floor, and children's furniture. Sometime after midnight a team of spattered, tired painters shared refreshments and looked proudly through the door at a transformed room. Washed curtains and a moveable divider made of brightly colored donated fabric on a wire gave us an inexpensive but cheerful and stimulating area for children to learn in.

Small churches are not known for their well-designed, well-appointed Christian education facilities. Sunday school rooms are likely to be used by a variety of groups, basement and attic rooms are pressed into service, or the kitchen and sanctuary double as Sunday school areas. With imagination, adaptation, and open minds, virtually any space can be at least adequate and probably favorable for learning and growing.

There are many creative options for dealing with the kinds of space problems often found in small churches. If the building problems are insurmountable, the utilization of nearby homes, other church buildings, public buildings, and the outdoors might offer suitable alternatives.

A different style of education can help answer space problems. For instance, the learning center approach can eliminate the need for several rooms. Classes are combined and can meet in one or two large rooms with different activities in different areas of the space. Learners are divided by interest more than age. Intergenerational learning experiences can also occur in one room.[6]

In sum, space limitation is not a legitimate excuse for inferior education. There are realistic solutions to virtually every space problem. And being small is no excuse for a littered, drab, depressing educational setting. No matter how small and how poor your church, there are people with unfinished cans of paint, people with extra fabric, people who can put on a supper to raise $100 to $500 to dress up a depressing area, and people with the imagination and gumption to transform the space that needs transforming.

WHO EDUCATES?

Who will be the teachers, leaders, guides, and gurus in your educational ministry? In an article on youth ministry in small rural churches, I noted the three criteria that are most important for workers with youth. They apply equally to people who work with children.

1. Someone who loves and respects young people and is loved and respected in return.
2. Someone who cares about the Christian faith and witnesses to it by his or her life, not merely with words.
3. Someone who has a contagious *joi de vivre*, or passion for life.[7]

Here is one approach for determining who should be working with a church's young people. Use a list of church members and check each person who fits the above three criteria. In other words, who are the good role models in the congregation? Even a small church should have several such jewels. From that list your teachers and helpers can be recruited.

You say, "That's fine, but only in large churches do you have the luxury of being able to be selective in who teaches church school." I say, "Not necessarily so." It is my experience that there will be enough teachers if:

- A church places a priority on education
- Teachers feel appreciated and needed
- A sense of "team" is developed, rather than teachers feeling they are being "cast to the wolves"
- Teachers are provided with helpful training and good resources
- Teachers are asked for a limited, specific time commitment (one quarter or one year), so that they will not feel they are being suckered into an endless commitment
- Teachers are encouraged to see their commitment as a learning and fellowship opportunity for themselves
- You are realistic in how many teachers you need (by combining ages, three teachers will make possible a preschool, an early elementary, and an older elementary class)
- Teachers are convinced they have needed gifts to offer

and that they can make a significant difference in students' lives

Who is going to train willing but inexperienced volunteers? Most pastors have had some Christian education training. Few know children and the art of teaching better than public school teachers. Most state or regional denominational offices have or can recommend good teachers of teachers. A large nearby church with a skilled lay or professional Christian educator would probably lend that person for a training event. Spend time together as a teaching staff helping one another problem solve and plan. If all else fails, try do-it-yourself training sessions using a resource like Donald L. Griggs's *Teaching Teachers to Teach*.[8] Good training and church support help make the difference between a church school where teachers and students go through the motions and one where morale is high, teachers are motivated, the atmosphere is electric, and learners become disciples and members of the family of faith.

Frequently churches relax and feel they have answered the "who" question when they have recruited the teachers. If we believe that each generation needs the others and the church is an extended family, then many more people must be involved. How about a rotation of grandparent-types bringing and serving cookies or carrot sticks weekly? How about the organist or choir director being asked to teach a new song? How about having the rug hooker, the carpenter, or the knitter teach the children his or her craft? How about asking those especially loving adults who claim they don't have any special gifts to join the staff as "lovers," as one small church calls them. These could be present to cuddle the shy child or to go for a nature walk with the one who is crying for attention by being disruptive. How about enlisting the shut-in to write birthday cards to all and "we missed you" cards to the absent? Christian education, properly conceived, is the responsibility and privilege of the *whole* church.

In a nearby small church there was a man known to most children as the Candy Man. Mr. Edwards was a house painter, a bachelor, and a man who loved children. Every Sunday for countless years he greeted all the children at the Sunday school door by name and with a piece of candy. No one asked him to do this. It was his way of loving little people. Mr. Edwards may have done more teaching and touched more lives than any of the official teachers in that church school. How can we enlist more people to fulfill the important role of the Candy Man?

HOW DOES EDUCATION HAPPEN?

When learners and teachers come together for Christian education at a specific time and place, a catalyst is needed to start a learning, changing process. Usually some materials or a curriculum is used to help grow Christian people and Christian community. In my part-time position as a Christian education consultant, the first question that is asked is usually about curriculum, yet it is no accident that here I have not mentioned materials. Curriculum is the educator's favorite scapegoat, yet it is not nearly as important as the total environment and the personality, preparation, and commitment of the teacher. It is only a set of tools, and no one ever hires a carpenter just because he or she has nice tools.

Yet tools or curriculum materials are important. In our search for an appropriate curriculum, we have over a period of years used five different curricula from different denominational traditions. After looking at many good, fair, and poor curricula, I developed the following checklist for evaluating curriculum materials. A good curriculum for a small church will—

_____ Be compatible with the prevailing theology and philosophy of the congregation
_____ Be attractive and appealing to the learners
_____ Be stimulating and rewarding for the teacher
_____ Present the Bible and church history as *our* ancestors and *our* story
_____ Have continuity and progression from subject to subject and level to level, so that after a few years the learner will have a solid biblical, historical, theological base

_____ Build self-esteem in the learner
_____ Use inclusive language and discourage gender stereotyping
_____ Use a discovery rather than a rote-learning approach
_____ Help students think and act creatively
_____ Build relationships and encourage Christian community
_____ Further students' integration with the rest of the church
_____ Be related to the world and experience of the learner
_____ Help students act on what they have learned
_____ Present the whole range of locales, ages, lifestyles, races, and cultures
_____ Be appropriate for combined grade and ability levels
_____ Have appearance, vocabulary, concepts, and activities appropriate for the age or developmental level
_____ Provide teachers with clear, creative, practical resources and instructions
_____ Use a variety of methods, activities, and materials
_____ Be useable with just a few (even two or three) students
_____ Be useable with limited supplementary materials, resources, and equipment
_____ Be affordable

The only way to evaluate curriculum is to see it and study it. Catalogs cannot be relied on. See what your denomination has. See what the neighboring churches use. A few curriculum publishing houses will send a sample or preview kit. A congregation might order one teacher and student sample for one age level of three or four different kinds of curriculum and base a choice on that sample.

Small churches need to be crafty buyers and active borrowers and scavengers. Post or print a list of needed supplies and see what the congregation and community can provide. Don't buy pads of newsprint, instead, ask the newspaper for the butt ends of their newsprint rolls, or the moving company for some of the newsprint they use in packing. In terms of equipment, a record player, a ditto or spirit duplicator machine, and a filmstrip projector are really useful. See what the nearby churches have in the way of equipment, filmstrips, and assorted resources and borrow from each other. See what your regional denominational office has in the way of resources to lend. Investigate what your public library, schools, civic groups, and YMCA or YWCA have that you can use. And don't forget the people resources in your church and community.

If a church's Christian education is thoughtfully and creatively conceived, if the congregation makes a strong commitment to it, and if it fulfills the following principles, it will be faithful and effective.

The Christian education program must be *wholistic*. The whole church, as it meets, eats, works, worships, cares, and serves, is where Christian education happens. It does not happen just in that appointed hour when the learners are down in the cellar or in the back room. The small church, where these functions tend to flow together, where by necessity space is used for various purposes, where by necessity people assume a variety of roles, is especially well suited to develop and practice a wholistic understanding of Christian education.

The worshiping congregation should hear and learn the song the elementary children learned. The church school will be more exciting when it participates in the mission committee's special project. The stewardship people should incorporate all ages into the concept and practice of stewardship. The Christian educators should and can seize every opportunity to connect the education endeavor with everything else that is happening. That is wholistic Christian education.

The Christian education program must be *individualized*. The small church has a great opportunity to have a big impact on individual lives, yet often it does not capitalize on this. Identify and respond to the gifts and needs of each person. See that each person has opportunities and responsibilities. People love to contribute to an offering plate passed by a five-year-old. Four-year-olds helped in our spring work day. See that each person is recognized on special days and for special accomplishments. See that each person is challenged to bear the fruit that God has seeded. If God numbers even the insignificant sparrows (Luke 12:7), surely the small church can creatively see that every person is known and needed.

The Christian education program must be *familial*. Large churches can talk about being a family, but a small church is family—though not always a healthy one. Families are combinations of people in relationship with and responsible to one another. The church school in its teaching can stress relationships and the Christian community. In its activity it can bring families, generations—the whole church —together. Family events like potluck suppers, field trips, an advent workshop, a spring Sunday school picnic, or a church progressive supper are naturals in small churches. In a time when divorce is as common as marriage, when thousands of miles separate relatives, and when there are more singles than ever, one of the most profound and needed ministries of the church is to offer people a family.

The Christian education program must be *ecological*. Whether urban or rural, we are all provincial. Christian education should help people learn and act on their interdependence with the rest of the world—the world outside the church. Not only is the church a family, but it is part of the family of humanity. We need to help people be part of the whole ecology.

The Christian education program must affirm the *tradition*. Our education programs must develop and communicate a continuous sense of the Christian tradition beginning with Abraham and begetting down through the ages to the saints, pillars, and characters here in our own churches, so that each person can be grafted on to the tradition. In a sense, this means opening the Bible so that we too become special people God speaks to and acts through. If we take the tradition seriously, we will emphasize and celebrate in memorable and fresh ways the church year—Advent, Christmas, Lent, Easter, Pentecost, and even All Saints' Day. The Bible will not be treated as a foreign tome, but as our own family biography. The lively Christian education program will affirm the tradition without being too traditional.

The Christian education program must be *Christian*. Ours is an incarnational faith—the Word was made flesh. It is not Christian education if we are just "teaching about" and "learning about." Christian education is not passing on knowledge, wisdom, or opinion, but introducing the Christ and making disciples. It is teaching everything that Christ commanded, and it is helping people to be Christ for others.

Finally, the Christian education program must demonstrate to our learners that faith should always be connected to *action*. It does no good to learn to pray for myself or my neighbor if I don't learn to *do* for myself and my neighbor. The small church should be especially good at this. It is small enough to find those whose faith is highly contagious and to expose them to others so intimately that they cannot help but catch it. And it is small enough to ensure that everyone will have opportunities to practice and reflect upon what has been caught. Every person from at least age three on up can be helped to love, give, do for, listen to, work with, make peace, and seek justice.

FOR DISCUSSION

1. How do you define Christian education?

2. Where and when does Christian education happen in your church?

3. How well does your church adopt people into your Christian family and nurture them in the Christian faith?

4. How could your educational ventures be more wholistic, individualized, familial, ecological, connected to the tradition, Christian, and connected to action?

CHAPTER 5

mission: not station to station but person to person

Eleven years ago the Warwick church budget listed fifty dollars for denominational missions, which the treasurer refused to send, believing it might be used for black power programs. Mission as it is perceived and practiced at our church is very different today. To illustrate better the shape and degree of change, here is a 1981 mission involvement summary, itemizing our mission action ranging from corporate and world to individual and local:

Our Christian World Mission (denominational)	$ 350.00
One Great Hour of Sharing	150.00
Heifer Project International	432.80
CROP (ecumenical hunger program)	344.87
Community newsletter	75.00
Deacon's fund (used to address special needs)	983.83
State conference fellowship dues	176.40
Andover Newton Theological School	25.00
Hartford Seminary	25.00
	$2,562.90

This was $600 more than the previous year and $2,500 more than was committed to mission eleven years ago. As a church we provided the following services:

Helping Hands (a local crisis-intervention service)
Sick Room Library (sick-room supplies loan program)

Pastor's and deacons' calls and counseling
Publication of community newsletter
Free use of building for community groups
Hosted Association mission education event

There are other less obvious but just as real ways our church touches and serves the world around us. One way is through community responsibilities. Many church participants were involved in town government and services: town moderator; town treasurer; town assistant treasurer; a selectman; 2 school committee members; 2 board of health members; 2 library trustees; a police officer; 2 assessors; chairperson of town finance committee. A significant percentage are employed in human service jobs: 5 teachers; 2 teacher aides; 5 nurses; a staff member of county planning office; a director of regional housing authority. Church members represent the church in community and in regional church responsibilities: editor and assistant editor of community newsletter; member of New England Heifer Project board of directors; moderator and 2 committee members of Franklin UCC Association; a person serving on conference task force. In other, less well defined ways the church is in mission to the community. For example,

- Members have caring relationships with neighbors, co-workers, and friends.
- Many members are part of community groups that provide services.
- Sharing of community and world concerns and prayers of intercession are an important part of worship.
- Church school reaches and serves the whole community.
- The youth group is the only activity in town for adolescents.
- The rummage sale is more for service than for profit.
- Caroling reaches out to community.
- Many see the church as a conscience for the community.

All these ways in which our church reaches out to the world around it can be called real or potential mission, but most of this mission does not show up in the mission statistics by which churches are judged. Mission is all that the church does beyond its own maintenance and membership boundaries which seeds and nurtures faith, joy, peace, justice, health, love, freedom, self-sufficiency, and discipleship here and throughout God's world. It is all the ways the Christian church follows Jesus' resurrection injunction to Peter to "feed my sheep" (John 21:15-17). By this definition our church is responsive in some areas of mission and weak in others. But the church in mission is far more than the programs it organizes and the church agencies it subsidizes. Mission is also what each Christian person does to seed and nurture faith, joy, peace, justice, health, love, freedom, self-sufficiency, and discipleship in daily life, as well as in far places.

Small churches are often criticized for using too much money and time meeting their survival needs. Perhaps this judgment is made because the definition of mission that many hold is too limited and too statistical. Even when the Warwick church had a budget of $1,500, no regular pastoral leadership, and only a worship service and church school, there was some concern for mission. As mentioned earlier, the reason they did not close the church was the conviction that it was vital to have a Sunday school in town. That is one manifestation of a sense of mission. With a broader and more biblical understanding of mission, even the most survival-oriented church will have manifestations of mission.

It has also been suggested that small churches are so good at and intent upon intimacy and caring for one another that they do not get around to mission. Perhaps it is true that some churches are little more than cozy clubs. People do comment on the intimacy and caring they find in this church, but our members have always been willing to reach beyond themselves. They have been open to visitors and new participants. They have been quick to help when people have been in crisis. They have been responsive to mission initiatives. Because a church is short on mission programs and appropriations does not necessarily mean it is short on the practice of mission.

Small churches, like most larger ones, have difficulty

"loving their neighbor" through social justice action, political involvement, and attacking the roots of the proliferating fundamental problems that plague these times. Thinking systematically is particularly difficult for smaller churches, where people deal with one another on a person-to-person basis. The tendency in Warwick, which is quite unwise, is to ignore the politicians and bureaucrats in Boston. Rather, like Don Quixote, we must have the cunning, courage, and stamina to tilt at the windmills which power the evils that abound.

Before a judgment is made about a church's commitment to mission, one needs to look beyond budgets and programs. In 1981 there was a mission commitment of $650 out of a total budget of $16,176, and only $350 of that was specifically earmarked for our denomination's mission program. These statistics could be used to label this congregation as unloyal to the denomination, insensitive to needs beyond its doors, and another typical survival-oriented small church. But that $350 is only the tip of our mission commitment iceberg. That amount is now $500 and will increase, as it has each of the last ten years.

In Chapter 1, ten keys to the transformation of the Warwick church were identified. Each is partly responsible for our significant commitment to mission. Mission themes (e.g., responsibility to our neighbor, connection with the larger world, stewardship of the creation) have been a priority in my ministry. There has always been a goal, dream, or vision in front of us. A church that has become very active has attracted active and talented people. Most important, mission has been defined, identified, and engaged in, in ways people can understand and be personally involved in. Any small church has as much potential to become a vital, mission-conscious church as this one is becoming.

Small churches can take mission seriously and be involved in mission effectively. Rather than being the wrong size for mission, the small church is just the right size for a style of mission that was characteristic of the early church and of Christianity through much of church history. The book of Acts and the Epistles give many examples of special offerings and actions to address special needs and of leaders and resources being used to assist other churches and people in need. If all this is true, why haven't small churches made big names for themselves as mission-conscious churches? There are several reasons.

Despite the rhetoric of the mission promotional materials, when you get to the bottom line, money and mission have been lumped together and become almost synonymous. The churches identified as having a strong mission commitment are the ones who send the most money or the largest percentage of their budgets to support the denomination's unified mission program. The myth is perpetuated that just as a church hires a minister to do their ministering for them, a church raises money so the denomination can do mission for them. What the denomination does is important. It is a necessary extension of the local church. However, the conclusion is often drawn that churches (generally the smaller ones) which do not send much money are not mission-conscious churches.

With money and mission so closely tied, and small churches being able to send only paltry sums, it is hard for them to feel as if their contribution makes a significant difference. Our $500 is a small drop in a huge ocean when compared to the United Church of Christ total support budget of over $11,000,000. Why get excited about something when you cannot make a significant difference, which only makes you feel more insignificant? Smaller churches have not been helped to see that their small contribution matters. Church World Service's hunger component, CROP, itemizes what $5 or $10 will do. And when we raised $3,300 for Heifer Project in 1975 we knew we had covered the stipend paid to our volunteer working for them, paid for an acre at their new headquarters ranch in Arkansas, and paid for a specified number of animals on a specific shipment. The clear message from CROP and Heifer Project is that even small contributions are appreciated and make a difference. And the result is that small contributions grow larger.

As illustrated by our former treasurer, the small church tends to feel distant from and distrustful of the national church. People in small churches—especially those in small towns—are used to knowing what happens to their money —that is, they know until it gets sent away in the form of taxes or denominational support. Richard G. Hutcheson Jr. suggests that the basic issue is the inevitable conflict between the increasingly corporate and bureaucratic denomination and its generalized mission program, and the local churches, which are voluntary organizations.[1] Voluntary organizations, and particularly smaller churches with limited resources, are inclined to put their money and their effort into ventures they know will do some good, rather than into ventures they know little about and have little say in.

Mission is seen in small churches (as well as in many larger churches) as more obligation than opportunity, more dues required than investment chosen. It is much like making one's bed is a duty parents require of children, rather than what I do to my bed so it will feel better when I climb in it at night. The denomination sends a letter telling the church what it should give (based on some formula) and the church (a) cheerfully responds, (b) dutifully agrees, (c) guiltily sends a compromise amount, (d) angrily ignores the letter and supports the mission project of its choice, or (e) does nothing.

Because mission is so often understood as what denominations do with your money somewhere else, churches —particularly small, rural churches—often have a very provincial sense of mission. Mission is out there, a long way away. When it is a long way away, we do not feel the hunger, see the injustices, smell the stench, hear the cry of the hopeless, or sense the urgency. Someone once observed that we feel more pain from a sliver in a finger than from the starvation of millions. Urban people are more likely to be confronted with the real situations or analogous conditions, but since rural poverty tends to be camouflaged, rural people often remain untouched. People can respond better to a need they feel.

A crisis in understanding is another reason mission does not get enthusiastic support. Some people are still under the impression that mission is missionaries converting the heathen. Most who share this conception feel no burning need to convert heathen. But if that is not the purpose of mission, what is it? People are not clear about the goal, the rationale, and the methods of the national church's mission program. In our smaller churches, which have been handicapped with less mission education and involvement, these questions have not been adequately answered. With partial answers, there has been partial commitment.

A prerequisite for mission consciousness is good and wise leadership. Small churches frequently have had the least experienced, most tired, poorest trained, and shortest-tenured clergy leadership. And since regional, state, and national lay leadership is usually chosen from the larger, "successful" churches, there generally are few if any lay people in small churches with the understanding to communicate the needs of church and society beyond the local church and society. One reason for the mission transformation in our church is that lay people have become involved with me in association and state conference activities. My commitment to the church beyond Warwick and to those less advantaged than us has been a factor. And a little-recognized factor here is that those who have challenged this church by asking "What are we doing in mission?" are people who came from churches that were doing more.

Carl Dudley writes, "Small churches are ... *culture-carrying congregations* who bring their identity from the past."[2] Later he writes, "As a culture-carrying congregation, their identity is not in a mission or a task."[3] Larger churches get their identity from their programs, the things they do. Smaller churches are known not by what they do but by who they are. A large church is likely to be known as "the church with the elderly housing program," while the small church might be known as "the friendly church." One is known for what it does, the other for what it is. However, that does not mean smaller churches cannot "do." Dudley concludes, "But the ministry and mission of the small church can be mobilized when they spring from the basic 'character' of a people who have a culture to preserve from the past and present to the future."[4] Their mission response will be most effective when it is an extension or fulfillment of who they are, rather than being prescribed from outside.

A rural church like ours can get excited about an agricultural program like CROP or Heifer Project. An urban church with many senior citizens can enthusiastically support a senior center. Why shouldn't a church's mission response mirror its particular makeup, expertise, and areas of interest?

Finally, some small churches *are* only survival-oriented. Psychologist Abraham Maslow's hierarchy of needs (discussed more fully in Chapter 6) applies here. Maslow suggests that we all have a progressive hierarchy of personal needs, beginning with the necessities of survival and culminating in the need to be "self-actualized." Some churches are only at the point of being able to fill the pulpit and pay the oil bill.

Many have suggested that churches which can merely survive should merge or close. It may be wise advice for some churches, but I'm wary of it. A decade ago the Warwick church would have been a prime candidate for this strategy. Survival-labeled churches may well be meeting genuine spiritual and social needs of remnant members. They may still have some redemptive or symbolic presence in their community. They may be dormant like a seed in the desert, needing only a little water to flower profusely.

In a survey I conducted of small churches in the Massachusetts UCC Conference, 11 of 93 respondents said they were "declining" (as opposed to "stable" or "growing"). Only 3 of 93 saw their future as "dismal" (rather than "uncertain" or "bright"). Many churches that others consider survival churches do not consider themselves survival churches. One wonders how many of the numerous "survival" churches which finally died would have flowered if someone with skill and respect had sensitively helped them regroup, review, and reorder themselves and offered them short-term financial support and long-term moral support. Many "survival" churches would commit themselves to and be transformed by mission if someone helped them discover they can be significantly doing mission, even if they do not have dollars to designate.

It is alarming to contemplate the ramifications of one false premise. The myth behind most of the above reasons

115

for low small-church mission commitment is that mission is money for use elsewhere. If that is all mission is, then of course the small church will have great difficulty being a mission-conscious church. However, if a denomination and its churches accepted and acted on a definition of mission like that which I offered at the beginning of this chapter, "Mission is all that the church does beyond its own maintenance and membership boundaries which seeds and nurtures faith, joy, peace, justice, health, love, freedom, self-sufficiency, and discipleship here and throughout God's world," the feeling about and commitment to mission would be vastly different on both the national level and the local level. Small churches would discover that even when they cannot afford to contribute significant sums of money to make an impact on life in Nigeria, for instance, they still can be a significant mission church as they contribute use of their building, their genuine spiritual support, and their time and energy to make an impact on the needs and opportunities of their community. And with the resulting growth of self-esteem, competence, and faithfulness, they will begin to catch a vision of being able to make a specific, significant impact in Nigeria or some specific somewhere.

STEWARDSHIP AND EVANGELISM

Stewardship and evangelism are two aspects of church life and Christian discipleship which properly belong in a chapter on mission but which people tend to think of as parts of the maintenance of their church. Churches talk about stewardship when it is time to garner support for next year's budget (or to make up this year's deficit). Churches talk about evangelism when they notice they are losing more members than they are gaining, when there are not enough contributors to support an inflation-swollen budget, or when the church across the street is growing. These are legitimate maintenance issues and will be addressed in Chapter 7. However, stewardship and evangelism are more than money-raising and "body-building."

Stewardship is recognition that as children of God we have been created and commissioned caretakers of the earth and all that is therein. God does not expect 10 percent of our resources. On the contrary, we are to be responsible and responsive in the use of 100 percent of our time, talent, and treasure. The distinction the church has made between the secular 90 percent that is ours and the sacred 10 percent that is God's is invalid. One hundred percent is God's and is sacred. One aspect of our total stewardship is how we participate in and support the life and mission of our community of faith. Yes, we do support the church to ensure its survival, but it is sinful to ensure its survival for the sake of its survival. Rather, the church must survive so that it may witness and serve.

Many small churches are quite good at stewardship. They have frequently been conservative in the best sense, that is, they have conserved what is valued and needed. Studies have shown that people in small churches give more and work harder than their large-church cousins. If our church is typical, people in small churches are proficient at recycling and conserving. Each Sunday after worship, bags of clothes are transferred from one car to another as parents pass on children's clothing to others with smaller children. It is amazing to look around our church fair and see how little of the merchandise is new and how much is homemade, homegrown, and recycled.

In rural small churches where many or most are gardeners or farmers, people have appreciation for the life processes of the seasons, the goodness of the soil, the importance of living with the natural laws, the virtues of cooperative activity, and the necessity of being responsible in the use of resources. Most small churches get a maximum amount of church out of a minimum amount of money. Rare is the church with a $130,000 budget which gets 700 percent more ministry and mission than this church gets with its $19,000 budget. Small churches can be the right size for stewardship.

Small churches have been criticized for their attitude and action, or lack of it, in the area of evangelism. Is it not logical that a small church which took seriously the Great Commission of preaching, teaching, and baptizing would soon no longer be small in numbers? Yes and no.

117

Yes, many small churches have probably chosen to remain small, for improper reasons. As a result of our size-conscious society, some have assumed that no one would want to join their insignificant band. Some have resisted growing because they assumed growth would mean a loss of intimacy and a dilution of power and authority. And some have not grown because they have not experienced much good news in the Good News which they feel compelled to claim and proclaim. There are small churches who say they cannot grow when in fact they have chosen not to grow or never gave it a thought.

But no, one cannot assume that a small church which is truly Christian will grow into a big church, or even that it should. Robert Evans, theologian at The Hartford Seminary Foundation, has convinced me that God calls churches not to grow but to be faithful and effective. Faithful and effective churches may or may not grow. Carl Dudley claims:

> Most small churches have already grown much bigger than they "ought to be." They look small only when compared with the larger organizational churches that flourish in metropolitan communities. . . . When compared to other kinds of caring groups, the small church is much larger than it "ought to be." When church size is measured by human relationships, the small church is the largest expression of the Christian faith.[5]

Dudley is articulating the honest fear of many dynamic small churches that growth might cause them to lose the qualities that enable them to be faithful and effective. Once in a while I hear the fear expressed that this church with sixty-five in worship is growing too large.

Many warm and vital small churches have not grown because they are situated in a context that is not growing and in fact may be declining. Warwick will always be a small town, and therefore our church will probably always be small, even though it has doubled its membership in ten years and continues to grow. Some very faithful and effective churches have not grown because they have sacrificed popular appeal for a prophetic witness to their community. Other warm and vital small churches have not grown because they have not learned that with effort and wise strategies they can grow and still have all the virtues of a small church.

As indicated before, evangelism is much more than adding new members. Evangelism is sharing and living the good news that God cares for each person and calls each to a life of discipleship. The first step in evangelism is converting the members already present. Today, particularly because of the influence of the so-called electric church, there is much more emphasis on growing in breadth rather than depth, quantity more than quality. Perhaps someday clergy will ask one another, "What kind of members do you have?" rather than, "How many members do you have?" A church that minimizes numerical growth and concentrates on converting the members who are present to a living and burning faith will probably attract new inquirers and disciples.

Another element of evangelism other than attracting new people is the church's influence on those on its perimeter. Jesus touched and influenced many people who did not show up on any membership roll. Around the edges of every alive church will be people who, for a variety of reasons, never actually become part of the body yet who receive redemptive benefits from the body and who contribute to the body. These are the people who donate to the steeple fund and the church fair, who send their children to Sunday school, and who come to the church for marrying and burying.

There are at least four types of people on the church perimeter. The "secular Christian" is so busy being involved and helpful in general that he or she hasn't found the time or rationale for getting involved in a church. The "crisis Christian" only feels the need for the church when either the person or the church is in crisis. An "osmosis Christian" gets enough religion or faith by association with wife, husband, or friend. The largest number of perimeter people are the "immune Christians," who have had just enough exposure to the germ of faith and discipleship to make them immune to a real case. The tendency is to consider all those who are not fully involved as barnacles on the ecclesiastical ship.

A wise and evangelical church will continue to minister to

119

these people in whatever ways are possible and let the Spirit of God work in its own mysterious ways. At worst the church will continue to influence and be available when it is especially needed. At best from the secular, crisis, osmosis, and immune Christians will emerge a few pearls who will be of great value to the trusting church willing to wait.

Yes, small churches can be evangelical. Those that are will grow in depth. Some will grow in breadth. They will continue to exercise a redemptive, healing influence in their environment. They will be faithful disciples of Christ regardless of their size.

THE UNIQUENESS OF SMALL-CHURCH MISSION

My thesis has been that everything is different in small churches—different because of size. People act differently, depending on the size of the group they are in. Groups function differently, depending on the number of people. A group of a given size will have the right number for some jobs and too few or too many to do other jobs effectively. People will expect different things of and respond in different ways to groups of different sizes. Paul Madsen missed the importance of size when he wrote: "The small church has no different mission than any other church of the land, regardless of size. It may use different methods to achieve that mission, but the mission of proclamation, fellowship, ministry, and service is the same for all."[6]

Perhaps mission conceived in the broadest terms will be the same for all churches, but more than methods will be different. Small churches will probably choose different needs, issues, and populations to respond to. Small churches will organize differently and will utilize different strategies and methods.

Also, the focus of a church's mission will differ according to its environment. Mission in an inner-city small church will be different from that in a suburban small church, which will be different from that in a rural church. Inner-city churches will more likely need to offer fellowship opportunities as an antidote to urban anonymity. Because of its size and setting, an urban small church will probably need to pinpoint such specific needs as school vandalism or a dangerous street crossing or language tutoring for a specific ethnic or population group. And it will generally focus on a limited geographical area—a neighborhood, street, or block. Thanks to its close proximity to a dense population, an urban small church's building and physical resources are particularly valuable mission tools. Often program and meeting space is needed more than money in the serving of a community, and churches usually have space that is underutilized. Also, urban small churches can be part of coalitions with neighboring religious and community groups in the tackling of larger needs.

Likewise, the suburban small-church mission will be shaped and seasoned by its locale. It will need to be cognizant of family needs and issues. Many suburban small churches will have members who are in influential positions in business, industry, social services, and government. The church should help these workers see they are part of the church's mission and then sensitize them to the issues, needs, and opportunities on which they can have an impact. These small churches can help people who have chosen the suburb for its insulated qualities to assume responsibility for less privileged peoples in less protected places. There will be community issues like zoning, housing, and schools, which the church can help its people act on.

And rural churches will need to customize their mission response. President Theodore Roosevelt appointed the Commission on Country Life in 1908. Their report included a reference to the country church: "The time has arrived when the church must take a larger leadership, both as an institution and through its pastors, in the social organization of rural life."[7] In contrast to the urban and suburban church, the rural church is generally at the center of the community—both geographically and socially. Its building is often a primary community meeting place. It is a center of communications for the community. Community leaders are frequently church members. It has the potential to be a strong influence at several levels of community life. Protection of the environment, farming concerns, rural poverty, zoning, and rural health care are a few of the rural issues the rural church can influence.

Many small churches have not placed a high priority on mission, yet they need to do so both because it is a biblical mandate and for their own sake. Whether the small church is at a rural crossroads or an urban intersection, there is a hungry and hurting world at its doorstep. Based on theory and practice, successes and failures, here are seven guidelines that can help a church that finds mission artificial and foreign discover it is natural and necessary.

1. *Through integration of mission with the other four basic tasks of the church, help each person claim and practice discipleship.* The learning in every church school class can end in action. Even a two-year-old can finger paint the cover for a get-well card for a sick person in the community. Community service and outreach can be woven into social events and fund-raisers. The sign board and exterior upkeep of the building communicate whether a church is open or closed, giving or taking. Small churches that are so good at caring for one another can be helped to extend that caring to those who do not come quickly to mind. Twice our deacons and I have conducted workshops on helpful hospital visiting.

It is vital that worship and mission be interconnected. Orlando Costas, a Latin-American evangelical theologian, writes, "Liturgy without mission is like a river without a spring. Mission without worship is like a river without a sea."[8] In worship we confess our failure in faithfulness and celebrate our activity on God's behalf, and we anticipate and prepare for the mission that awaits us. As we are in mission, we discover the need to return to worship for new wisdom, courage, and collegiality.

Because the small church is small, its mission can be and must be the work of the whole people and not just that of the clergy, the mission committee, or a special-interest group. As we have recognized before, the small church can work as a whole. For one mission project, we invited the whole congregation—including children—to take one, five, or ten dollars and invest it (as in the parable of the talents) and return the results. The proceeds were celebrated by all in worship. Move mission into the mainstream of the church in recognition of the biblical and theological fact that the church is mission.

2. *Make the sense of mission organic to the nature of your people,* and make it more than money raised and sent. Our church has been effectively involved with Heifer Project because its agricultural emphasis makes sense to our agriculturally minded people. If your congregation has an abundance of older people, develop a senior citizen program or utilize their grandparent instincts in a children's program. Two questions should be answered and brought together: What is our nature and what are the needs? People get excited about mission when they are personally involved, using their own experience and skills, and able to relate personally to the need they are addressing.

3. *Call people to and train them for loving their (next-door) neighbor.* Help people understand that mission is not only what the church does collectively and through the denomination but also what they do individually in their own arena—the home, school, factory, office, neighborhood, town, or city hall. Hendrik Kraemer clearly states:

> Everything in the Church and in the world revolves around the so-called "ordinary member of the Church." For in him must become somehow visible that the Lordship of Christ over the Church and over the world is not a fairy-tale or a gratuitous assertion, but a reality which "bites." . . . The total activity of the Church in its worship, its preaching, its teaching, its pastoral care, should have the purpose of helping the "ordinary membership of the Church" to become what they are in Christ.[9]

The "ordinary members" need to be helped to see how the definition of mission applies to their own daily living as neighbor, citizen, employee, employer, student, friend, spouse, parent. At the same time, people need help in seeing that if mission begins at home, it does not end there.

One year for our annual meeting, I visited each adult and

youth in the church at his or her place of work or home, where I took a photograph of each at work. I wrote a script and presented a slide narration program using the slides to illustrate who we were, what we did, and some of the significance of our lives. A small church can help each person identify his or her particular sphere of potential mission and a strategy for carrying out that mission, and then commission each person for his or her work in Christ's name.

4. *When person-to-person mission is not meeting difficult or pervasive needs, develop strategies and programs that will help people meet them.* There is a lesson about small-town small-church mission which I had trouble learning. I love to plan programs. I have learned well that many problems are systemic in nature and need to be attacked systemically. My urban-suburban background and education have taught me well that if there is a community problem, one surveys the community and then designs, implements, and promotes a program to counter the problem. While this is frequently right and true, it is often difficult in a small community or small church.

Recently I helped our Mission Committee survey the community to ascertain local needs and to suggest a variety of projects or programs. Surveys were mailed twice to every home in the town. Only a handful were returned. Did the poor response mean apathy, hostility, forgetfulness, a bad survey, ignorance, satisfaction, procrastination? Perhaps each of these played a role. But the factor I often overlook is the feeling in this community that it is not programs that meet needs, but people.

However, there are times and problems that require programs. Earlier I described our free community newsletter, which is the only means of communication that reaches every home. Though only five years old, it is a valued institution. Warwick is part of an economically depressed region. Almost all local people work outside town, and only a trickle of the money they earn stays in the community. We are now printing a "Warwick Yellow Pages" which will encourage our local economy. Each home is called to solicit listings of services, home businesses, and products. This is a free service and is distributed without charge to each home in town. These are two examples of programs that work because they are personal and meet real needs. The small church needs to be a detective who ferrets out needs, a switchboard that connects helpers and helpees, and a mad inventor who designs better mousetraps.

5. *Educate the congregation to the larger, more systemic needs and issues which are at the root of the needs and issues our people experience or perceive.* Small-church people are often blissfully ignorant of the "principalities and powers" of our complex world. The issues of world hunger, the arms race, multinational corporations, and so on are exceedingly difficult to grasp yet exceedingly important for Christians to address. Groups like Bread for the World, Common Cause, and denominational program agencies can help local church people counter the simplistic ideas of groups like the Moral Majority. We all need help in cutting through the rhetoric, the technical language, and the conflicting claims so that we can determine faithful and effective Christian responses to major problems.

It is tempting to leave the big problems to big government or big business—those who supposedly understand them —while we concentrate on the problems we face daily. This is a serious mistake. Arthur Simon points out:

> A single action by Congress or one decision by the President can undo—or multiply—many times over the effect of all our voluntary contributions combined. To make an offering in church for world relief and quietly leave the big decisions up to political leaders only encourages them to make *wrong* decisions.[10]

6. Not only educate, but *work for a world consciousness.* Help people find ways to love their distant (in the ghetto and across the seas) neighbor. Help them discover that the gospel requires justice as well as love. Help them find pragmatic and effective ways to follow Jesus' direction to go into all the world. In Warwick we have drawn people out of the confines of this community and helped them be aware of the larger world.

Denominational mission resources can help with this. We have hosted missionary speakers and foreign students. World events become part of our time of concerns in worship. A church could develop a correspondence and yoked relationship with a foreign church. A church might ask its denomination to help it select an international project that would minister to a specific person, family, church, or town. It is possible to express a world consciousness on a person-to-person basis.

An old legend tells of a knight riding his horse down a dusty road, who saw a tiny sparrow lying on its back in the road. The knight stopped, leaned down and asked, "Sparrow, what are you doing?" The sparrow answered, "Holding up the sky!" The knight scoffed and the sparrow countered firmly, "One does what one can. One does what one can." The diminutive size of a small church faced with the mammoth problems of a mammoth world is no excuse, since it can and must do what it can.

7. Even when one does what one can, there are some things a single church—large or small—cannot do. It is important continually to *lead the small church into a covenantal mission commitment with other churches,* both denominationally and ecumenically. Smaller churches often have a difficult time claiming their rightful place in the family of churches, but it is doubly important for them to do so. First, there are leadership, resources, ideas, and support to be gained. Second, small churches have important contributions to make to other churches. They have a unique perspective that larger churches need to hear. Through their person-to-person style they can remind larger compatriots that no matter how complex the problem, it is persons that God calls the church to serve and love.

However, the primary reason for uniting forces is that there is a mission that is quite possible when each part of the unified Body of Christ works as it should (Eph. 4:16). We are part of the interchurch covenant when we do what we can financially *and* when we contribute the skills, insights, and commitment present in each congregation. There is a

126

natural tendency in smaller churches to feel they are so short on financial and human resources that they cannot share any for the collective work of the larger church. Yet not to share is a slow form of suicide.

Part of good mission and stewardship is recognizing what we have to contribute to the covenant besides, or in addition to, money. A small church can share its building as a meeting site or retreat center for other churches. It can collect clothing for Church World Service or some other organization. It can donate labor and salvaged materials to work projects. It can share what program resources it has. And so on. One of the primary styles of New Testament mission was one church sharing with another. That should still be part of our mission style.

THE POSSIBILITIES FOR MISSION

Sprinkled throughout this chapter are a variety of needs, methods, and projects that a congregation could take on. The possibilities are limitless. For example: Make church-owned empty land available for "victory gardens," or plant a garden and give the produce to gardenless people. Offer the building as a site for health clinics and programming by public service groups. Organize after-school and adult education programs for the community. Develop a food pantry, thrift shop, food co-op, and other cooperative services and exchanges. Form a continuing relationship with a nursing home, sheltered workshop, halfway house, or penal institution, and visit, nurture friendships, provide services, invite residents to worship and other programs, and advocate for them with government. We all are surrounded by needs and opportunities for service and sharing God's liberating Good News. The question is not what can we do, but what will we do.

For a church to be faithful and effective in feeding, clothing, visiting, healing, welcoming (Matthew 25), or in bringing good news to the poor, liberty to the captives, sight to the blind, freedom to the oppressed, and the proclamation of God's redeeming love (Luke 4), it must be visionary and

127

discriminating, as well as loving. A mission church must be able both to see what is and to envision what might be. It must also be able to decipher out of the world's clamoring what needs and opportunities are most important and most appropriate for its available personnel and resources. And it must then give itself in love. The gospel demands not piety but love.

The following suggestions and questions can help a church assess needs and opportunities, set priorities, decide what it is and is not equipped to do, and gear up for action.[11]

Do some Bible study together. Some pregnant passages are Amos 5:21-24, Matthew 5:44-45, Matthew 10:16, Matthew 25:37-40, and Ephesians 2:13-14. Ask of each passage and one another three questions: What is God saying in this passage? What might God through this Word intend for us as this people in this time and place? What might happen if this church were to incarnate-live this passage?

Carefully and creatively identify the needs and opportunities that surround you. Brainstorm what needs you as a group perceive. Read your newspaper. Go to your library, chamber of commerce, and city or county planners and get the latest data about your community and area. Pile into cars and do a windshield survey of your community (get off the beaten path). Interview town or city officials, police chief, judge, welfare workers, school administrators and teachers, area health agencies, newspaper editor, ad hoc community groups. Respectfully interview your "street people" (youth, those who "hang around"). Instead of being tedious, the above surveying will be both fascinating and revealing.

When it is time to set priorities, ask: Which needs are most pressing? Which are not being addressed by anyone else? Which would your church have most energy for? Which could your church have significant impact on? If Jesus Christ were in your church, which need would he push you toward?

Look at what resources you can bring to bear on the need. Will your whole church or a significant part help? Do you have or can you raise whatever funds are necessary? Are there people or groups in your community who would join forces with you? How can you use your building, or do you need to borrow or rent space? How much leadership, and what kinds, do you need? For how long will you be committing yourselves?

There are some general principles to consider. Choose a need or project that is pressing and significant. Involve as many people as possible. Use every way possible to inform (continuously) the church and community about what you are doing and how they can help. Have little jobs for the people who are leary of big ones. Be relatively certain you can accomplish what you are attempting. Evaluate as you go and afterward. Before, during, and afterward, pray and worship.

In a small church there are things that cannot be done, tasks that are too large or complex. However, because of smallness there are things that we can do, a mission we can effect. The potential for intimacy and immediacy makes possible a kind of mission that is difficult in larger settings. Philip Hallie chronicles the remarkable story of how hundreds of Jews and refugees were saved from Nazi arrest by the Rev. André Trocme and his church and the town of Le Chambon in France. Hallie tells how Trocme enabled in the Le Chambon church the kind of intimate caring and commitment which he had once experienced in a Protestant youth organization and which is the spirit of mission in the small church at its best.

For the rest of his life he sought another union, another intimate community of people praying together and finding in their love for each other and for God the passion and the will to extinguish indifference and solitude. From the union he learned that only in such an intimate community, in a home or in a village, could the Protestant idea of a "priesthood of all believers" work. Only in intimacy could people save each other. And because he learned this well, the struggle of Le Chambon against evil would be a kitchen struggle, a battle between a community of intimates and a vast, surrounding world of violence, betrayal, and indifference.[12]

FOR DISCUSSION

1. What is your church's definition of mission? Is it narrow or broad?

2. In what ways are your people engaged in mission?

3. On the continuum from survival to mission (scale of 1 to 10), where would you place your church?

4. If you tailored your mission to the unique nature of your church, what might it look like?

CHAPTER 6

caring: a genius
for growing real people

The splendid velveteen rabbit with pink sateen lined ears
sat wedged in the boy's Christmas stocking with a sprig of
holly between his paws. For a long time he was one of many
toys in the nursery. He felt commonplace among the many
expensive toys, mechanical toys, and modern toys. One day
the Rabbit asked the old, worn Skin Horse:

"What is REAL? . . . Does it mean having things that
buzz inside you and a stick-out handle?"

"Real isn't how you are made," said the Skin Horse.
"It's a thing that happens to you. When a child loves
you for a long, long time, not just to play with, but
REALLY loves you, then you become Real."

"Does it hurt?" asked the Rabbit.

"Sometimes," said the Skin Horse, for he was always
truthful. "When you are Real you don't mind being
hurt."

"Does it happen all at once, like being wound up," he
asked, "or bit by bit?"

"It doesn't happen all at once," said the Skin Horse.
"You become. It takes a long time. That's why it doesn't
often happen to people who break easily, or have sharp
edges, or who have to be carefully kept. Generally, by
the time you are Real, most of your hair has been loved
off, and your eyes drop out and you get loose in the
joints, and very shabby. But these things don't matter

at all, because once you are Real you can't be ugly, except to people who don't understand." . . .

The Rabbit sighed. He thought it would be a long time before this magic called Real happened to him. He longed to become Real, to know what it felt like; and yet the idea of growing shabby and losing his eyes and whiskers was rather sad. He wished that he could become it without these uncomfortable things happening to him. . . .

That night, and for many nights after, the Velveteen Rabbit slept in the Boy's bed. At first he found it rather uncomfortable, for the Boy hugged him very tight, and sometimes he rolled over on him, and sometimes he pushed him so far under the pillow that the Rabbit could scarcely breathe. . . .

Weeks passed, and the little Rabbit grew very old and shabby, but the Boy loved him just as much. He loved him so hard that he loved all his whiskers off, and the pink lining to his ears turned grey, and his brown spots faded. He even began to lose his shape, and he scarcely looked like a rabbit any more, except to the Boy. To him he was always beautiful, and that was all that the little Rabbit cared about. He didn't mind how he looked to other people, because the nursery magic had made him Real, and when you are Real shabbiness doesn't matter.[1]

Margery Williams' winsome story expresses the essence of what the small church is best known for—its knowing and caring for one another. It just happens to you, over a period of time. You become. It hurts sometimes, but you usually don't mind much. Often people who break easily, who have sharp edges, or who have to be carefully kept choose not to go through becoming Real. Because attention is on other matters, people do grow a little loose and shabby, and un-Real people tend not to understand. Becoming Real can be uncomfortable, especially at first, and many long for an easier way.

Carl Dudley observed that small churches are only the appropriate size for the members to know one another personally. My experience is that the small church is the appropriate size for all the things that are essential for being the Christian church. However, the small church does have a unique genius for caring for persons, for becoming a

Christian community, for helping people become and remain real persons. This remarkable attribute is usually more intuitive than intentional. This is not to say that there are not insensitive, hostile, or cruel small churches or people in small churches. It is to say that they are the exception more than the rule. Let us see what makes real people, what there is about small churches that accounts for this special genius, and how it can be made more pervasive and productive.

What is a real person? What are we trying to help people become? Jesus said, "I have come in order that you might have life—life in all its fullness [John 10:10,TEV]." Certainly Jesus is talking about realized life. The word salvation has been used a lot in the Christian church, especially in its evangelical wing. While people tend to equate salvation with being saved, few are aware of the root of the word, which is *salvus* and means being healed or making whole.[2] Other words that connote realness are authentic, centered, organic, shalom, or at peace. Real is the opposite of false, synthetic, illegitimate, and unrealized.

Elizabeth O'Connor illustrates the desire to make people real with the story of Michelangelo pushing a huge piece of marble down the street. A curious neighbor called from his balcony and asked why the sculptor was working so hard to move that huge rock. Michelangelo stopped to wipe his brow and answered, "Because there is an angel in that rock that wants to come out."[3] Unless we picture ourselves as a finished product, there is in each of us an angel waiting, wanting to be fashioned and finished.

Abraham Maslow, American psychologist, writer, and teacher, developed a theory of how the angel in us emerges. It is known as Maslow's "hierarchy of needs." He suggested all our thoughts and actions are attempts to meet needs we have, and that these needs are in a logical sequence in which the basic needs must be met before we can concentrate on others. A simplified version of Maslow's hierarchy looks like this[4]:

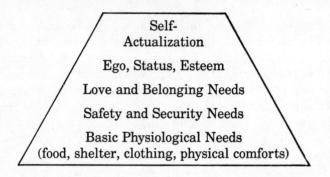

According to the theory, we are not able to worry about safety needs until our most basic physical needs are met, or about love and belonging until physical and safety needs are met, and so on. The higher we move in the hierarchy, the more real we become. As life in small churches is related to Maslow's hierarchy, we can see more clearly why it has a genius for growing real people. At each level of the hierarchy, small churches can and frequently do make significant contributions to our realization.

Basic physiological needs. Of the $2,500 that this church invested in some form of mission last year, almost $2,000 was used to meet basic physiological needs here or elsewhere (e.g., Heifer Project agricultural development, CROP hunger action, One Great Hour of Sharing disaster relief, gifts by the deacons to people in crisis). When I was ill one summer, about twenty church members cut, hauled, split, and stacked our winter firewood supply. Whenever there is a fire, the victims are inundated with furniture, clothing, and other necessities. When everyone knows everyone, each person's basic physical needs are recognized and can be addressed. Small churches are known for looking out for the physical needs of the members and those within their sphere of influence.

Safety and security needs. Many people turn to or return to the church to meet some of their safety and security needs.

Some people want their infants baptized as a form of "life insurance." Membership and attendance go up in times of war, depression, and insecurity. It is frequently the minister to whom the insecure, unstable, or vulnerable turn. The attention the church gives to people at life-crisis times helps meet their safety and security needs. Just as people turn to their biological family when threatened, they also turn to their small-church family. And small churches can be particularly adept at taking in and caring for one of their own.

Love and belonging needs. Once a person's physical needs and security needs are met, attention begins to turn outward. In the second creation story (Gen. 2:4-24) a man was formed from the ground and given life. God planted a garden to provide the man with food—the physical necessities. He was put in the Garden of Eden—a secure environment. But then the man was lonely. Beasts and birds were created, but he was still lonely. A woman was made, and man and woman cleaved together in mutual companionship.

To be human is to need to be in relationship with special others. Integral to relationship is loving and belonging. Dudley calls the relationship of intimates a "caring cell." Larger churches tend to be composed of a collection of cells with many other people on the fringes. Smaller churches tend to be one larger cell. "When compared to other kinds of caring groups, the small church is much larger than it 'ought to be.' When church size is measured by human relationship, the small church is the largest expression of the Christian faith."[5] The small church has a special aptitude for letting people know they belong.

Ego, status, esteem. In this stage in the hierarchy there is often contradiction. A large problem of many small churches is low morale. By osmosis they have picked up from the culture and larger church the feeling that they are insignificant because they are small. In relation to the world around, small-church people do not get much ego, status, and esteem satisfaction. On the other hand, everyone in a small church can be someone. Everyone knows you. You are missed when absent. You are needed to keep the ship afloat and on course.

People who have never had the opportunity to be a leader or to make things happen can be a leader and a productive person. Dietrich Bonhoeffer describes the importance of each person's contribution to both the individual and the community:

> In a Christian community everything depends upon whether each individual is an indispensable link in a chain. Only when even the smallest link is securely interlocked is the chain unbreakable. A community which allows unemployed members to exist within it will perish because of them. It will be well, therefore, if every member receives a definite task to perform for the community, that he may know in hours of doubt that he, too, is not useless and unusable.[6]

As people discover they are not useless, they can have their ego, status, and esteem needs partially met, and as these churches establish their rightful place in the larger world more of these needs can be met.

Self-actualization. Another word for self-actualization is self-fulfillment. This is where the angel really emerges from the rock. The parable of the talents illustrates God's intention that every person become all that his or her potential promises. Each person is created a gifted individual. "A primary purpose of the Church is to help us discover our gifts and, in the face of our fears, to hold us accountable for them so that we can enter into the joy of creating."[7]

A small church is a fine laboratory for identifying, experimenting with, and combining the raw elements. It is a stage where each person is critical to the unfolding drama. The opportunities are plentiful, and the needs beckon reluctant volunteers. A pratfall can be taken without great consequences. Efforts will be accepted, because small-church people are more concerned with persons than with the product. One of the priceless benefits of my eleven-year pastorate in Warwick is the satisfaction of seeing the remarkable growth, or "self-actualization," of many people and the positive change in almost everyone. These people acknowledge that our church, through its opportunities, nurture, and encouragement, has been responsible for much of their growth. People need to be cared for at each level, and small churches have a unique potential and opportunity to do so.

CARING CREATES COMMUNITY

In our world full of strangers, estranged from their own past, culture and country, from their neighbors, friends and family, from their deepest self and their God, we witness a painful search for a hospitable place where life can be lived without fear and where community can be found. . . . It is possible for men and women and obligatory for Christians to offer an open and hospitable space where strangers can cast off their strangeness and become our fellow human beings.[8]

One result of caring is that people become more real. Another result is that trust and interdependence build, and a sense of community develops. "Community refers to the communion of humans, that is, the unity in which human differences remain. The differentiating of human uniqueness and the movement toward solidarity occur together."[9] Community is a commonplace word and a most difficult reality. Small churches do not easily develop a sense of community, but the more people there are, the more difficult community becomes. Elizabeth O'Connor, after years of successfully working at developing community as part of the small, highly disciplined Church of the Savior in Washington, D.C., writes about it:

This is the most creative and difficult work to which any of us will ever be called. There is no higher achievement in all the world than to be a person in community, and this is the call of every Christian. We are to be builders of liberating communities that free love in us and free love in others.[10]

The theme and reality of community is found throughout the Bible. The biblical understanding of the Christian church is that it is a caring community in mission to the surrounding world. Our smaller churches have the capacity to realize the biblical view of the church. Paul wrote: "God has so composed the body . . . that the members may have the same care for one another. If one member suffers, all suffer together; if one member is honored, all rejoice together [1 Cor. 12:24-26]." To care for another and to be in community with others means simply to be with and for the other(s) in good times and bad. There are some biblical motifs that can help move us toward that difficult but possible reality of community.

Luke 10:38-42. This is the story of Mary and Martha. After a hard day of walking and talking and being with people, Jesus is invited to the home of two sisters. Perhaps Mary and Martha were with Jesus that day and the invitation to stop was spontaneous. Anyway, Martha needs to see that everything is just right. She scurries about picking up the house. The good dishes and guest towels must be put out. Water must be fetched from the well and more fish from the fishmonger. To Martha, hospitality was a matter of preparedness, organization, and propriety. Casual Mary, however, ignored her frantic sister and chose to be with, rather than to do for. The way the house looked, even the food that was on hand, was less important than enjoying the opportunity to be together.

Small-church caring and hospitality tends to be more like Mary's than Martha's. The priority is on being together rather than impressing each other. People would rather potluck than banquet. Meetings are as much for catching up and telling stories as they are for conducting business. What some consider gossip, small-church folk consider necessary information. People who are not comfortable with informality, bantering, and "wasting time" talking, will not be at home in a small church.

Caring moments in the small church are rarely by appointment, in the counseling hour, or as part of an agenda. They are more likely on the street corner, in the parking lot, over the phone, on the way out of church or over coffee, or when the pastor stops by. Community will happen less in planned "koinonia" groups than after the funeral, at the work bee, during the sharing of concerns, or when the prodigal returns. Mary would have been at home in a small church.

Luke 15:3-6. The parable of the lost sheep is the story of the shepherd who discovers one sheep is missing, leaves the other ninety-nine "in the wilderness," and goes searching for the lost one. Would a shepherd really leave the flock defenseless in the wilderness to look for one sheep? Is this an example of the foolishness of God versus the practicality of humanity?

In a larger church it is easier to get lost and to stay lost. The shepherd in this church is more likely to stay with the flock. There are more than enough sheep to tend, needs to meet, and chores to be done.

This is a small-church parable. The sheep that gets lost is missed immediately. The flock will feel incomplete without the wanderer (although sometimes a flock will purge an unwanted member of the flock). The shepherd will know the runaway's habits and favorite haunts. If the sheep has received personal attention (as sheep in small flocks do) it will soon miss the flock. When the prodigal is found, there will be rejoicing that a member of the family has returned, that the flock is again complete.

The parallel breaks down if we assume the pastor is the shepherd and the laity are the flock. When the small church works as it should and is a community, all will look out for the others. Today's shepherd may be tomorrow's lost one. But in community there is always a rescue squad who cares.

John 13:1-15. This is the poignant foot-washing episode. Jesus was a rabbi, evangelist, healer, and prophet. He was also pastor of a small church of a dozen or so people. Has there ever been a small church more frustrating than his? They slept when they should have been awake. They didn't want Jesus to waste his time with children. They fought over the power positions in their "church." They misunderstood. They were frequently faithless. They squabbled a lot. Jesus must have had extraordinary patience.

John tells of a supper Jesus shared with his little church. It was customary for guests to have their feet washed, usually by the house servant. Rather than wait for the servant, Jesus got up from the table, wrapped a towel around himself, and began washing feet. Simon Peter was shocked and embarrassed that Jesus should stoop to wash his feet. Jesus answered, "If I do not wash your feet, you will no longer be my disciple. . . . You, then, should wash one another's feet [John 13:8, TEV].

Here is another graphic illustration of caring and community among small numbers. In churches where ministers are sought first for administrative and oratorical gifts, who washes the feet of people? In contrast, Jesus' model of ministry requires care of both soul and sole. Caring is concern not just for spiritual needs but also for social, emotional, and physical needs. In washing the disciples' feet, Jesus is, among other meanings, helping the disciples feel at home. He is being the consummate host. Nouwen writes: "The minister . . . is a host who offers hospitality to his guests. He gives them a friendly space, where they may feel free to come and go, to be close and distant, to rest and play, to talk and be silent, to eat and to fast."[11] The host prepares the space and creates an environment where people can feel safe and take risks, be ministered unto and minister to.

In community there is both sin and grace, brokenness and hope. As Jesus' community shared this event, Judas' intention to betray was known to Jesus. Even in their intimate group there was misunderstanding and self-serving. Yet as Jesus modeled a style of community in which each serves the other and none is superior to the rest, he demonstrated the possibility of shared grace and hope in community. "Hospitality becomes community as it creates a unity based on the shared confession of our basic brokenness and on a shared hope."[12]

The foot-washing story suggests not only the style and content of caring, but also the identity of the care givers and community builders. Larger churches often prefer and can afford to hire their care givers. "One of the great heresies of the contemporary church is the idea that the primary role of the ordained person in a congregation is to exercise a ministry of caring on behalf of the others who are responsible for his or her hire."[13] Smaller churches cannot as readily hire professionals to care for them, and maybe they prefer the do-it-yourself method. Jesus directs the disciples to wash one another's feet. It is the job of all, not the job of the slave or the professional. Jesus demonstrates that it is the job of the leader to model caring and to train the cadre of foot washers.

Small churches are particularly capable of being hospitable to and caring for the whole person. Small churches are the right size for community, and their people generally are looking for community. They should be ready, then, to do what Elizabeth O'Connor says they are supposed to do.

> The primary purpose of the disciplines, structures of accountability, and mission of the Church is to build life together, to create liberating communities of caring. To each of us is given a gift for the building of a community of caring, a community in which we can learn to embrace our pain, and to overcome all those oppressive inner structures that would keep us in bondage and make us protective and anxious for our own futures.[14]

As was demonstrated with education and mission in small churches, caring also is not the task of a few or a specific program among many programs. It is fundamental to and integrated throughout the whole fabric of the small church. It is not the sole responsibility of the greeters, the deacons, the calling committee, or the minister(s), but part of the job description of each member. It is more likely to happen in small churches, where people have more than one responsibility, may have greater commitment, and think personally more than programmatically.

What would it be like in a small church if caring was characteristic of each aspect of church life? In worship there would be as much emphasis on the horizontal (person to person) as on the vertical (God to person, person to God). Confession would be for failure in relationships, more than naughty thoughts and deeds. Sharing of concerns and prayers of intercession would have a special place and priority. Sermons would be personal, interpersonal, and life-centered, rather than general, impersonal, and abstract. The person preaching would be visible and touchable, rather than a torrent of words spilling from a mask. Choir members and other worship participants would be selected as much for what might happen for them as for what they can produce. Visitors, lost sheep, and prodigals would be welcomed and included. Worship would strive for a balance between intellectual and emotional, personal and interpersonal, spiritual and temporal. It would be seen as a training event and community-building exercise for the congregation's caring ministry. Touches, hugs, laughs, and tears would be commonplace and appreciated. The ancient concept of the sanctuary as a place of refuge would be revived and practiced.

In education there would be at least as much emphasis on learning to live in community as on learning about the Bible. Teachers would be selected for their gifts of warmth and compassion more than for their religiosity. The needs of the learners would be more important than getting through the lesson plan. Being learned and good would not be stressed as much as being just and loving. The goal would not be religious scholars, but whole, healthy, caring Christian disciples. Generations would be brought together to learn from one another.

Mission would not be defined either as giving money to hire surrogate missioners or as a program of the church. It would be defined as caring on an interpersonal and universal scale. It would promote a style of life which is universally active, loving, peaceable, and just. The Good Samaritan who cares for whoever is in need would be held up as a model for the whole laity. Each person would be helped to see that he or she can do something. Those who are more comfortable giving than receiving would be helped to accept the love of others. Those who are accustomed only to receiving the care of others would be asked and helped to give. Those with personal problems, conflicts, or neuroses would be counseled and cared for so that they become givers.

Even the maintenance of the church must be infused with caring. Chapter 7 defines maintenance as everything the church does so that it can worship, educate, care, and serve. The quality and quantity of a church's caring will be increased or retarded by the way the building is maintained,

142

the budget is determined and supported, the church fair is organized, meetings are conducted, conflicts handled, and so on.

A church does not have the choice of caring or not caring. Neither does it have the choice of only caring. On one hand, a truly Christian church that does not care is as improbable as a fire without warmth. Perhaps there can be a religious institution that is uncaring, but that cannot be true of a Christian church. When it ceases caring, it ceases being a church. On the other hand, if it is concerned only with caring for one another it will also cease to be a Christian church. Instead, it will be simply a therapy group or a social club. For a church to be the church, there must be a commitment beyond itself. Bruno Bettelheim writes: "I am convinced communal life can flourish only if it exists for an aim outside itself. Community is viable if it is the outgrowth of a deep involvement in a purpose which is other than, or above that of being a community."[15]

Caring can also be uniquely difficult in a small church. For some people caring is as difficult as one would think making love is for porcupines—at best it is done very carefully. The assumption of intimacy and common knowledge is a source of problems. Frequently people will hide their needs and problems for fear "everyone" will know their business or they will lose the respect of others. Some people could be more open if there was more anonymity.

Some people seem to think the pastor is omniscient and will certainly know that Aunt Hilda is in the hospital, when the news has not made its way along the grapevine. It must be frequently repeated that the pastor can not be expected to call unless he or she is notified. If you are the pastor, ask those who are particularly close to the pulse of the community to let you know what people expect you to know.

Sometimes so much is known about a person that a normal caring response is withheld because the person is considered a hypochondriac, always into trouble, no good, or the like. Familiarity may not breed contempt, but it might make a helper more leary than if less was known about the troubled. Because we know people so well in the small church we can sometimes match people who can be helpful to each other. And in other situations we may need to refer people to help outside the parish because of the familiarity factor.

The caring nature of a small church sometimes grows to mythical proportions. Some count so strongly on the mythical caring that the imperfect caring which is extended is judged inadequate. The vision of becoming a truly caring community must be continually held up, while at the same time people are reminded that we are flesh and blood, imperfect people.

Another caring problem in small churches is conflict. In most loving families, people fight, and in most loving churches, people will disagree and fight. Speed Leas and Paul Kittlaus stress that conflict is one part of caring for another.

> If one doesn't care about the other person or what he is doing, one will not be motivated to fight with him. If one doesn't care what other people are doing or saying within the church, one will not be interested in them and will avoid confronting them. To the extent that one does care about the other, and the relationship is significant, one will be able to be in conflict with the other.[16]

Small churches have a reputation for being prone to conflict. If conflict is a function of caring, and caring is characteristic of small churches, then small-church conflict can be expected. That does not make it easier or more pleasant. The test of the quality of caring in a small church is not whether there is conflict but how disruptive and destructive it is allowed to become. Often the lay people who trust one another enough to fight are less appalled by a fight than is the clergy, who are satisfied with nothing less than pure, unrealistic *agape* (Godlike) love.

The prevalence and power of a church's caring can be enabled and expanded. Some ways have already been implied. Here are additional strategies:

1. When you are looking for a pastor, make a gift for caring high on your list of priorities.

2. Make sure everyone knows every member's name and knows about everyone. Use name tags occasionally or when anyone new is present.
3. Eat together a lot. Use any excuse for a potluck.
4. Sell boxes of get-well cards, greeting cards, and the like, as a way of encouraging people to remember one another.
5. Conduct a workshop on hospital and nursing home visiting, to help people conquer their fears.
6. Be particularly attentive as a church to people in times of crisis. Perhaps an astute and sensitive person could be formally or informally designated the "crisis manager" to see that people are remembered, supported, and assisted.
7. Have a church retreat with plenty of time for sharing and discovering the beauty of one another.
8. Do not call people together or call on them only when you want something from them, like time or money. Call them together sometimes purely to play or to celebrate.
9. Involve your church in a mission project that includes opportunities for caring to happen and community to emerge in the process.
10. If you are the pastor, do more pastoral calling than you have time to or like to. You cannot care for people you don't know, and you do not know people you haven't been with on their own home turf.
11. Persuade and train lay people to make pastoral calls.
12. Find reasons to get people into one anothers' homes. Say things like, "To save on the electric bill, let's rotate Christian education committee meetings in our homes."
13. Decorate and furnish your building so people will want to linger rather than flee. More caring happens after worship than at any other time in our church.
14. Find creative ways to help your children develop their caring aptitude. They are never too young to care.
15. First and last, find at least a core who will do Bible

study and pray faithfully, thankfully, and caringly for one another, others in need, and the whole community. Where there's honest prayer, there is care.

For many people, caring is the bottom line as they assess a church. Warren Hartman's significant research with people who have dropped out of Methodist churches revealed:

> The most frequently mentioned reason on their list was their failure to feel that they were accepted, loved, or wanted. They felt that they did not belong and that others in the church and church school did not demonstrate any real love and concern for them.[17]

Many recall with nostalgia some experience in some "little brown church in the vale." Many see small churches as warm, cuddly remnants from bygone days. They are not always warm and cuddly, but neither are they an anachronism. The small church is potentially a lifesaving oasis in a desert. In an impersonal, computerized, commercial world, it is one of the special places where we can be real, cared for, caring, and in community.

In our small churches it is possible for us to:

- Call by name those who are merely a number to the Internal Revenue Service, the Social Security Administration, the U.S. Postal Service, and the motor vehicle department
- Offer shelter to those who are buffeted by winds of change and transition
- Offer family to those who feel alone and orphaned
- Make those who feel superfluous feel they have something to offer
- Develop faith in those wandering the desert of secularity
- Care in a care-less world

FOR DISCUSSION

1. On a scale of 1 to 10, how caring of those inside is your church? Of those outside? What ages, types, persons get forgotten?

2. Identify times when *you* were especially cared for by your church.

3. Look at Maslow's hierarchy (page 134) and discuss how your church cares at each level.

4. Does your church relish, avoid, or manage conflict?

5. How might caring and community be increased in your church?

CHAPTER 7

maintenance:
homemaking or housekeeping

For a Christian church to be faithful and effective, it must attend to the five basic tasks of worship, education, caring, mission, and maintenance. The first three can be joined under the label "ministry." The church then becomes a 3M company—ministry, mission, and maintenance. Maintenance is everything else a church does so that it can ably worship, learn, care, and serve. The various dictionary meanings of the word maintain can be related to what a church must do to maintain itself. Church maintenance areas are: leadership, facilities, organization, finances, communication, growth, morale and conflict, planning, and outside relationships (denominational, community, ecumenical).

A church that pays no attention to its maintenance will soon have no church to pay attention to. Its worship will lose its focus and coherence, its education will be mediocre and aimless, its caring will be haphazard and fragile, and its mission will be directionless at best and nonexistent at worst. However, a church that gives all its attention to maintenance will be a well-oiled machine going nowhere.

Many critics have accused small churches of being so preoccupied with institutional maintenance and survival that they fail to pursue or fulfill their other mandates. And many small churches are criticized for not being able even to handle maintenance well. One denominational official writes:

> In many denominational and interdenominational conferences, church leaders have concluded that any church of 200 is marginal. Such a church will have difficulty in adequately supporting its minister, providing essential maintenance of physical property, and carrying on an educational program. Very little will be left for mission in the community or in the world. The church will be forced to turn inward simply because the fight to survive will absorb the energies, the financial resources, and the time of the members. . . . Regardless of the number, a small membership means a church that is hard pressed to maintain an organization and committee structure that permits it to participate fully, completely, and in a satisfying way in the life of the denomination and the community. Such a church will have an inadequate budget in most instances, which in turn may lead to a high rate of turnover in pastors. Even if a pastor were content to accept the salary that would be offered, he or she still would not be content to accept the limited program of service and ministry that would be possible on a starvation budget.[1]

From the outside the Warwick church might look like the kind just described. It will probably never be able to pay an adequate full-time salary for a full-time minister, have a fully equipped facility that is ideal for all purposes, have an income that provides for all it would like to have, and look and function like ecclesiastical experts think a church should look and function.

However, because this church has carefully and wisely understood who it is and who it is called to be, and has sought to shape itself and act according to its own uniqueness, it is a well-maintained church. Our organization adequately functions so that our work is coordinated and good decisions are made and acted on. On a budget of $19,000 (for 1982), we can pay for what we need and invest in people and needs beyond ourselves. Our building is modest but adequate, and it enables our ministry and mission. The atmosphere is positive and supportive. With only seventy members, there are enough workers. With a half-time minister, a one-and-one-half-day-a-week seminar-ian, no secretary, and no janitor, almost everything gets done that should be done. This church handles its mainte-nance so that it can faithfully and effectively go about its ministry and mission.

Just as a small church can be the right size for worship, education, mission, and caring, it can be the right size to maintain itself satisfactorily. However, a small church will probably find it difficult to be the right size for maintenance if it is saddled with a big budget, a big building, or a big program. It will probably fail at maintenance if it tries to live up to standards and specifications established by others. It must pioneer its own style and procedures and have an accurate understanding of its limits and potential. Follow-ing are learnings, ideas, and insights related to nine main-tenance areas: leadership, facilities, organization, finances, communication, growth, morale and conflict, planning, and outside relationships (denominational, community, ecumen-ical).

LEADERSHIP

The key maintenance question is whether the task is "homemaking" or "housekeeping." The difference is critical. A housekeeper cleans, arranges, manages. A housekeeper's duties are clear-cut. The homemaker is concerned with family relationships and morale, with the health and securi-ty of the members of the home, with maintaining a warm and open environment, with their lives outside the home, and with their past and future.

Larger churches need and look for administrative or managerial qualities in potential leadership. The tasks are to build, coordinate, lead, and keep house. Smaller churches are in need of homemakers who can nurture, encourage, and enable the family members in their relationships, growth, and ventures. In larger, program-conscious churches, the task or job to be done tends to take precedence. In smaller churches, relationships and people are generally more im-portant than the job. Carl Dudley suggests that small churches want their pastors to be "lovers" rather than professionals or specialists.[2] They want leaders who are human, approachable, and responsive. These qualities are needed in lay leaders as well. Thus, what is needed in small churches are homemakers more than housekeepers.

Small churches are likely to have many people with real, although often disguised, leadership abilities. Lay leadership has developed by necessity because of the sparsity of members and frequently because of the lack of clergy leadership. Our church could not have gone pastorless for decades without committed and able lay leaders. The small-church leadership problem is not lack of leadership but turnover, training, burnout, and commitment.

Frequently there is little turnover in leadership. In many churches it seems as if Mrs. X has been the treasurer, moderator, or Sunday school superintendent forever. Turnover does not occur, because "no one else will take it" or "I don't want to hurt her feelings" or "I know more about it than anyone else." I've suggested that the small church has the characteristics of an extended family. Family therapist Virginia Satir writes, "What happens so often is that family members got literally stuck with one of the roles, and then that role takes over their whole self."[3] In the same way, long-tenured, dedicated souls in the church become so synonymous with their role that they fear losing the role would mean losing their identity. Perhaps some of those who cling to their roles would not need to if their church could clearly show them appreciation and respect for who they are and what they might do, as well as for what they are doing.

In this church Charlie Morse served a long and valuable tenure as moderator. Four years into my pastorate he graciously suggested that someone else be nominated. That made it possible for new leadership to emerge and develop, and it allowed him to assume other roles in the church. A subsequent bylaw change requires a turnover in officers every four years (or two terms for multiple-year offices). This ensures and results in leadership being shared and expanded. We follow a principle of asking virtually everyone to serve on a committee or in an office, and almost all say yes. Turnover results in greater interest, new leadership, shared power, the development of new abilities, and no stagnation.

Generally the only training is on-the-job training or experience brought from the secular world. On-the-job training only teaches how to do it the way it has always been done. Relying on experience gained in the secular world has some benefits, but it often results in the church acting like a secular organization rather than with faith, compassion, and commitment. A small church could be ignited and transformed by asking a denominational person who understands small-church ways, or a competent small-church leader from another small church, to lead a training workshop. Two, three, or a dozen churches could go together in such an event. The church lives and flourishes by the utilization of amateurs, but rank amateurs are another matter. If you require training for your people, they will know the job is important.

Burned-out and turned-off leaders result when leadership is not rotated and responsibilities are not shared. When we select teachers, we ask for a one-year commitment, no longer. People know they have the right to say no or not now. Seldom are people asked to reconsider when they decline. The result is that few decline. One of our leaders commented, "There is a tremendous respect when we've had to say 'no, I can't.'"

There are other reasons for burnout, besides overwork. Sometimes people want out when they feel they have been investing themselves in a thankless job, a job for which no one says "Thanks a lot." People want out of jobs that offer them nothing. Volunteers should be encouraged to set personal goals for themselves in responsibilities they accept —what they want to learn, gifts they want to develop, experiences they want to have. Depending on how it is approached and defined, any church job can be either debilitating or stimulating.

The best way to ensure lack of commitment in your leaders is to suggest "Oh, it's easy" or "It won't take much time" or "Anybody can do it" or "We couldn't find anyone else." If you ask for commitment, provide training, show appreciation, encourage personal growth and reward, and do not make it a "till death do us part" job, your volunteers will be committed. Also, volunteers should be provided with adequate tools for doing their job—a decent typewriter, good curriculum, or suitable music.

Does the nominating committee function as a slot-filler, arm-twister, or matchmaker? Frequently people are nominated because "he's done it for years," "she won't say no," "she will have hurt feelings if we don't," or "everyone else is too busy." If the committee members see themselves as matchmakers, they might ask questions like:

- What gifts do we suspect she has that this position would develop?
- Whose unconventional ideas might help us look at this in a new way?
- What new experience or responsibility would he enjoy?
- Would this position help her move into the mainstream of our church?
- How can we utilize his abilities without sapping the energy he devotes to his important community service?
- How can we utilize the ideas, energy, and abilities of our children and youth?

These questions help simple maintenance chores become opportunities for ministry and mission.

What if there just are not enough people for all the offices and jobs? Some denominations specify or urge an extensive and complex organizational structure. Madsen notes that "the usual denominational program is predicated upon a church of some four or five hundred members."[4] This question reminds me of Jesus' assurance that "the sabbath was made for man, not man for the sabbath [Mark 2:27]." This could be paraphrased "The structure should serve the church, not the church should serve the structure." The key questions are: How many jobs must be done if a church is to be faithful and effective? How many people are really required to get the job done? A small church could be very faithful and effective if it took the five tasks (worship, education, mission, caring, and maintenance) and recruited two people for each. Those plus a pastor or lay leader coordinating their work could carry on an exciting and comprehensive ministry and mission. And that is two fewer people than the first church—Jesus and the twelve disciples —had in its membership.

What about clergy leadership? The next chapter is devoted to lay and clergy ministry, but something should be said here about styles of leadership. What is not needed in a small church is an executive director, expert, or boss. What is needed is a hybrid of a catalyst, juggler, priest and prophet, cheerleader, Ann Landers, traffic cop, best friend, janitor, and a bit of P.T. Barnum. Seminaries are not very good at developing these qualities in their students, so what the new minister cannot do instinctively, the church will have to nurture in their minister or do itself. Perhaps the best plan is for laity and clergy to do what they can and trust the Spirit for the rest. After eight years in a small, out-of-the-way church, a Maine minister described the satisfaction he felt about the way responsibilities were managed in his church:

> Really I'm serving the ideal church. I know it's not a large one, but the people are great workers, and that means a lot to me. The custodian manages the building; the music committee manages the choir; the deacons manage the benevolences; and the trustees manage the finances. All I have to do is manage myself![5]

FACILITIES

Many have poked fun at the church's "edifice complex." When the early church, which met in homes to break bread, is compared with the real estate, buildings, and belongings of the contemporary church, all that can be said is, "You've come a long way, baby!" But which way?

Most churches are identified primarily by their building ("the pretty stone church on Fourth Avenue"). And many churches are served well by a building that provides space and context for ministry and mission. Many others have drowned in red ink with an albatross of a building pulling them under. For some the church building is just a building, a structure where people meet, but for many others the building is an album of memories, a bulwark of security, and a beacon of hope.

One cannot generalize about small-church buildings. Some small churches are housed in small buildings that fit well. Other small but once large churches are dwarfed in mammoth buildings suitable for an earlier day. Each has real problems and real opportunities. Some small churches are handicapped by a building that has little more than worship space, but they are blessed with lower costs. The other extreme is the small church with a vast amount of space, whose energy and upkeep costs are staggering; in this case, however, excess space can be utilized for a wide variety of church and community uses. And there are many small-church buildings like ours, which are both economical and functional.

An ecclesiastical tragedy of our time is the number of churches that have disbanded largely because of the cost and inappropriateness of their buildings. There are at least two such churches in Massachusetts. Like the dinosaur who could not adapt to a changed environment, they dwindled and died. Could their death have been avoided if they had affirmed the possibilities of smallness, unloaded their outdated buildings, and searched for more suitable housing?

Our church made a providential decision back in 1936 to buy a house rather than to go into debt for a traditional church building. The style, arrangement, and economy of our building has a great deal to do with the nature of our church. The same opportunity comes to many churches, often as a result of a crisis. Each year church buildings burn down, outside interests offer to buy expensive-to-maintain church edifices, churches federate or unite or share buildings and abandon their "white elephants," and federations break apart, leaving one church homeless. Also, a few brave churches fearlessly evaluate their building requirements before they are faced with a crisis situation. All these churches have the opportunity to rethink the nature of their church (a building or a people), the focus of their ministry (the maintenance of a building or being the Body of Christ), and the locus of their mission (what happens in the building or in the world around). They have the option to use insurance, sale, or invested monies to subsidize creative and visionary decisions about the kind of space that is really desirable and necessary.

There are several alternatives for small-membership churches that are making a building decision. One is to buy or rent a home or office building of suitable size and condition. Our experience has been that there is no better place to build a sense of family than in a home. And our house, while lacking the familiar steeple or belfry, has attracted and charmed visitors. It costs us little and accommodates our various uses.

There are other alternatives. Some small churches have merged and consolidated in one building. A very small or very committed church might go nomadic, like our earliest church ancestors, and utilize their own homes or offices. Just as many people are buying smaller and more economical cars and houses, many churches have traded down to a smaller church building that another church has given up or outgrown. And others have succumbed to ego needs and traditional practices and erected expensive new structures. Before a church makes a serious building decision, it would do well to study the first verse of the catchy Avery and Marsh song "We Are the Church,"[6] which goes:

> The church is not a building,
> The church is not a steeple,
> The church is not a resting place,
> The church is a people.*

If an existing church building is appropriate for the church, or even if it is a dear and memory-laden building that people will not or cannot part with, there are decisions and actions that need to be considered. Can it be made more energy efficient? Innumerable articles, books, and experts can be consulted. Could the building be put to better use by inviting other groups and services to share the space and

*Copyright © 1967, 1969, 1970, 1971, 1972 by Richard K. Avery and Donald S. Marsh. International copyright secured. All rights reserved. Used by Special Permission of the Publisher.

costs? Can it or should it be refurbished or adapted so that the very young are more at home, the handicapped are not further handicapped by their church, the hearing- or sight-impaired can hear, see, and participate better? Can or should it be face-lifted so it is more inviting from the outside? Can or should the building be made more functional and flexible by such things as installing folding doors, moveable seating, and the like? Are volunteers being utilized as much as they might be in cleaning, upkeep, alterations, and even in major building improvements? The use of volunteers is good stewardship, a community-building strategy, and a ministry to people's need to be needed. Particularly in smaller communities, this is a way to involve and utilize those on the perimeter of the church who chose not to be involved in other ways.

Finally, when a church is thinking about its facility, it should consider all the "signs" posted around the building, which are usually invisible to the regulars. Some of the invisible signs in your building might be:

- Steep entry stairs that say, "People in wheelchairs, on crutches, or who have a serious heart condition or emphysema should go elsewhere"
- An ill-equipped or nonexistent nursery that says, "You and your children aren't welcome here until they are four"
- A shabby exterior or interior that tells others,"Our church is not a priority for us"
- Restrooms short on paper and long on odor, which clearly tell visitors, "Those of us who know better don't spend any longer here than we have to"

The church building is the first communicator to visitors and neighbors about the people inside. What does it say? What changes are necessary so that the signs say what the people intend?

ORGANIZATION

In the area of organizational structure, small churches are much maligned and misunderstood. They appear archaic and inefficient. At the end of the Carter administration, Vice-President Mondale was assessing how "the system" of government might work better:

> First of all, I would relax a little bit in terms of this emphasis on "working better." In other words, my old friend Hubert [Humphrey] used to say you can read the Bible from the first word to the last and read the Constitution all the way through, and you can read the Magna Carta and you will never see the word "efficiency" mentioned once.
>
> Our system is not supposed to run on time. When issues are serious, when they are controversial, they are supposed to simmer for a while. They are supposed to slow down so that the public is engaged.[7]

If this is true of the mammoth federal bureaucracy, it is especially true of, and proven by, our small churches. They may not be punctual, business-like, or efficient, but they work. And the lack of orderliness is part of their genius. The small church can function and thrive without being efficient because of its size. Even back in the nineteenth century Georg Simmel wrote:

> A group upon reaching a certain size must develop forms and organs which serve its maintenance and promotion, but which a smaller group does not need. On the other hand, it will be admitted that smaller groups have qualities, including types of interaction among their members, which inevitably disappear when the groups grow larger.[8]

The smaller church is distinguished from its larger cousin by being able to:

- Allow as much time for "family" interaction as for business
- Give everyone a say, rather than having spokespersons speaking for others
- Have decisions made or reconsidered simply and directly, rather than being passed through channels or up a chain of command
- Make decisions by consensus, rather than by majority rule
- Work as a whole, rather than in subgroups

A United Church of Christ church-planning manual offers both an understanding of how organizations function and a style of organizational life which make sense especially for small churches. It suggests that a healthy organization accepts and allows for three components in its life: "myth," "belief," and "norm." The "myth" is not a fairy tale but the memory and sense of identity upon which the group relies for its meaning. The "beliefs" are the common theological ideas, covenant, and stated purposes and goals that the church professes. The "norms" are the programs, politics, and ways of doing things. "A healthy organization moves from a feeling about who it is (myth), to an articulation of those feelings into statements of what it is for (belief), to actions and behaviors which express its identity and purpose (norms)."[9]

The smaller the organization or church, the more coherent and common the myth. The smaller the group, the more likely a mutually acceptable statement of belief. The smaller the body, the greater the possibility that all or most of the participants will behave or act in common, consistent, or compatible ways.

The manual proposes a style of organizational functioning called "provolution." Provolution means to turn ahead or turn to the future. The emphasis is on using the group's energy and creativity to focus on future possibilities. This is in contrast to problem-solving methods that dwell on present concerns without the guidance of a future vision. A group with a provolution orientation will stress the importance of affirming rather than using each member, utilizing the strengths of each rather than lamenting weaknesses. It recognizes that a sense of community is important and that within any group there is a wealth of talent, wisdom, and resources.[10]

In small churches where there is low morale, where problems seem overwhelming, where there is a sense of insignificance, and where the temptation is to overtax the membership, this organizational style makes sense. A small church will be healthy when it recalls the goodness in its memory and myths, when it knows what it believes, and when it acts together to realize goals and visions. With this orientation each person will matter, problems will be manageable, and smallness will be an advantage.

When this organizational theory is used, workers and groups are helped to set goals and look to the future. Each person is helped to identify and take responsibility for his or her gifts that can be used in ministry and mission. Problems are seen not as stumbling blocks but as stepping-stones. When groups meet, time is spent getting in touch with one another, in community-building and in worship, and in identifying specific objectives and plotting strategy for reaching them. The church acts as an Exodus people pilgrimaging to a promised land.

Small churches come in several organizational forms. Kenyon Butterfield, writing in 1909 about country churches, asserts that "wherever possible, superfluous churches should be eliminated, and all existing churches united for many practical co-operative ends."[11] Since then the desire for practicality and efficiency has led to the closing of many smaller churches and the formation of many kinds of ecclesiastical hybrids. Alan Waltz lists the following options: circuit, consolidated church, federated church, yoked field, cluster, enlarged charge, extended ministry, group ministry, and larger parish.[12] These are often viable options for some churches.

There are pros and cons for entering into a cooperative arrangement with one or more churches. When salaries, buildings, and resources are shared, the economics are more manageable, and this can be good stewardship. Also, the pooling of human talents and efforts can yield greater accomplishment. And the kind of negative competition that often results when there are too many churches serving one population is not healthy or defensible. Interchurch cooperation is commendable when it is organic and beneficial.

However, the impetus to get churches yoked, federated, and clustered has come more from outside powers than from within congregations. And it has been urged more for reasons of efficiency than faithfulness.

In most denominations in the 1960s there was an active attempt to "deal with the small-membership church" by promoting the organizational schemes listed above. Often a key motivation was to reduce the number of "marginal" and "inefficient" units and to simplify the administrative and programmatic tasks of the denomination.[13]

Many of these efforts have not worked, through no great fault of the participants. Dissimilar congregations are frequently urged into a marriage simply because they are small, poor, and geographically close, which by themselves are not legitimate reasons. Such "marriages" end in divorce. Just as a bride and groom must be compatible, are helped by a common heritage, should share a common commitment and vision, need to make careful preparations, and should be prepared for periods of great stress, so must congregations contemplating living together or marriage. Such liaisons often result in members dropping out because they do not feel at home, or people moving to the back because they no longer feel needed. Any church considering such a joint venture ought to study carefully the ideas and implications of Douglas Walrath's chapter in *Small Churches Are Beautiful*.[14] They should also participate in a thorough "premarital counseling" process with a competent church/marriage counselor.

One model that deserves more attention is the one which has worked so well for this church and for me. This model maintains the identity, integrity, and memory of the individual church, while finding creative ways to resolve the economic pressures and to share resources with other churches. The heart of our model is a bi-vocational ministry by the clergy. "Bi-vocational" is one of several terms used to identify a minister with more than one source of income. The greatest expense for most small churches is the minister. That is still true for this church, but the expense, since it is only a half-time salary, is both manageable and beneficial for the church. A bi-vocational style of ministry has many advantages but is underutilized. It allows the pastor to have a livable income and real involvement in the world outside the church. It allows the church to have the kind of professional leadership it cannot afford and to live on a budget it can afford. It allows the church to have its "own" minister, rather than a loaner. Because the pastor's time is limited, it forces the congregation to maintain a lay ministry alongside the pastor's. This church is far more faithful and effective than it was during its two periods of federation. And it may be more faithful and effective than if I were their full-time pastor.

MONEY

Money is frequently perceived as a life-and-death matter in small churches. James Lowery wrote in 1974, "We now estimate $25,000 as the minimum for congregational survival, and $40,000 necessary for real effectiveness."[15] If these figures are adjusted for inflation, they would be in the neighborhood of $45,000 and $65,000 in 1982. How is it that our church, more than surviving, was thriving in 1974 on $8,400, and is even more so in 1982 on $19,000?

Madsen claims, "There is an irreducible minimum budget for all churches. . . . If they attempt to maintain an adequate building for worship, education, and community gatherings, plus a paid ministry, a basic budget will be required regardless of size of membership."[16] There are two different questions here. How much money is required to carry on faithfully and effectively the tasks of worship, education, mission, caring, and organizational maintenance? How much money is required to maintain a tradition-imposed or inherited church building, fully compensated clergyperson, or other assumed expenses?

A small church could satisfactorily fulfill the basic tasks of the Christian church, even today, on little or no money. Of course, the people would have to be incredibly responsible and creative in giving their time and talent in their shared ministry and mission. However, almost all churches have or want a church building and substantial clergy leadership, and this does cost money, although Lowery's figures seem highly inflated as prerequisites for viability.

Money is *not* the issue in faithfulness and effectiveness. Instead, the issues for a church are:

- Are the perceived needs necessities, optionals, or frills?
- Is the church funding maintenance for the sake of survival, or for maintenance, ministry, and mission?

162

- Will the bottom-line figure be a snap, a challenge, or a debilitating burden?
- Are personnel being fairly compensated for the expected time and talent? And what is fair? And what if the church cannot afford to be fair?
- How will the church underwrite its perceived need?
- Where will the necessary income come from? Endowments? A broad base or a disproportionate few supporters?

The time-honored, larger-church approach to stewardship is based on every member canvasses and loyalty Sundays. Carl Dudley suggests, "The caring cell does not respond well to every-member canvass, every-member pledging, and year-round budgeting."[17] He believes this is because people know one another too well and the approaches feel "canned." They are not ways members of a family support one another. One midwestern rural pastor told me his church could not set the budget until the crops were in and sold.

Our experience has been that a budget is appreciated and needed. It is a way not only of planning but of objectifying our commitments and priorities. A one-sermon and one-letter approach to pledging, and the promise that only the treasurer knows the amount of the pledge, has worked here. There has been neither the interest in nor a need for a canvass, but we carefully communicate the validity of each budget item. Our experience is that when people know the need, are part of the ministry, and are asked to be responsible in their giving, they are good and faithful stewards.

There are many critics of the small church's rummage sales, food sales, auction, and strawberry festivals. Most small churches, including ours, rely on projects to raise a significant part of their budget. A traditional fair, apple pie sale, and auction, and one or two other annual events account for about one-fourth of our income. Critics say these kinds of fund-raisers take too much energy and time away from mission and that the church should support itself. There is some merit to these charges.

However, when planned and conducted reasonably and thoughtfully they have many virtues. At the various sales people can get good, needed merchandise at low prices. They can use their money twice—to get a product and to support a service. They are a means of recycling resources—clothes, bits of material, attic treasures, and so on. They provide people who have little money to give an alternative means of helping their church. Whether people are working or just attending, it gets them out and involved. As people have become involved in fund-raisers, we have seen them discover or develop rusty or hidden gifts. Fund-raisers are a terrific way of involving people on the fringes of the church. Community-building can happen in a natural and substantial way as people work together. They are a wholesome form of needed local recreation. And in our case they make possible church school, ministry to the hospitalized and shut in, local worship, maintenance of a building that serves the community, a youth group, spiritual growth, a community newsletter, mission in Warwick and the wider world. These events can be agents of grace, creators of community, real forms of stewardship, a means of mission, and more.

The various forms of denominational subsidy for small churches can be life-saving or life-sapping. They can create dependency or help a church become independent. Three times in ten years we went to our state conference for a small grant (the largest was $500), each to subsidize a new initiative. Each time the denomination said yes. Each time the money was for a limited period. The result is a much stronger church that feels trusting and appreciative of its denomination.

COMMUNICATION

A Sunday school teacher asked a child which parable she liked best. Jennifer answered, "I like the one where everybody loafs and fishes." Even in the single-cell church, noted for its closeness, communication needs constant attention. Just as Jennifer misheard, communication in small churches can be garbled and misheard or not heard at all. In fact, communication is especially important in small churches. First, it is important because everyone expects to know about everything. Since they expect to know, it is incumbent on the church to see that they do. Second, because people assume everybody knows everything, messages sometimes are not passed on as carefully as they might be in larger groups. And third, in a "bigger is better" society, small churches must overcome the prevalent prejudice that since they are small what they do must be insignificant.

Two of the most essential tools of ministry are a good typewriter and a mimeograph or spirit duplicator. Every church needs this equipment, and a good church supper or two will provide them. They make it possible to communicate beyond what is passed by word of mouth. But just as what is said is often not heard, what is printed is often not read. The church's printed word must be concise and coherent. Whether it is creatively and attractively presented will determine how it is received—as a special message or junk mail. Our community newsletter, with both a church and community section, is a valued vehicle of communication.

In smaller cities and towns the newspaper is an effective way of communicating with parishioners and potential parishioners. Newspapers will print almost any news release that is well written. If people regularly read about a church in the newspaper, they will guess that something unique is happening there. Radio stations are obliged to broadcast public service spots. Let them help get the word around.

A "party line" is another strategy for seeing that people are informed of meetings, issues, sick folk. If one calls six and they each call six, thirty-six homes get the message quickly. The sign board in front of the building not only gives the schedule but also tells whether the same old thing is happening or something fresh and interesting.

Sunday morning is a time for praising God and passing the word. People have said that if they miss worship they don't know what's happening in town. Announcement time, a sharing-of-concerns segment in worship, bulletins, bulletin boards, and the coffee hour are ways of making the church the news room for the community. What is said is frequently not heard. So say it both verbally and visually, and say it frequently.

Churches seek growth for legitimate, quasi-legitimate, and illegitimate reasons. In this largely bad-news culture there are many people in need of the Good News which is the best news available. There are churches so infused with this Good News that they exude zeal and contagiousness. They know it cannot be preserved or hoarded. There are other churches that seek growth for the sake of institutional preservation. People are recruited to shoulder some of the work and financial responsibility. And there are churches that seek growth for the same reasons board players seek monopolies or tycoons seek wealth—for power and prominence.

The issue is not whether a church grows but for what purposes it seeks growth, and what the consequences are for church and recruits when growth occurs. When growth is not carefully conceived, or is pursued for institutional or egotistical reasons, the result can be loss of intimacy, dilution of faithfulness, and confusion between quality and quantity. It is a sin either to fetter the Good News or to shred, sweeten, puff, package, and peddle it like Sugar Pops.

Growth has not been an overt goal for our church, yet it has grown by about 150 percent in the time our town has grown by 25 percent. Why? It has grown because it has tried to be, and others have found it to be, a hospitable place with friendly people. People have been attracted by its faithfulness, liveliness, and commitment to service. Others have come because of its rich mix of ages and outlooks. Some are here because they feel needed and appreciated. People become part of groups that meet their spiritual, social, and emotional needs, and that has been true here. But there are others who have *not* chosen this church because of its intimacy, or its expectations of strong commitment, or its small size, or its many children, or its informality, or the theology of its leadership.

For a church to grow it must know who it uniquely is, be willing to share itself, and then do it. And there must be people wanting to make a match with such a church. A church willing and desiring to grow should specifically ask itself who it uniquely is and then identify what it has to offer, and then check these perceptions with new members, recent visitors, neighbors in the community, and dropouts. The second step is to develop and implement strategies for embodying and sharing these qualities. For example, if the building is particularly appealing, invite community groups to use it and hold regular open houses and public programs with tasty refreshments. If there are many silver-haired saints, perhaps the church could specialize and prize a ministry with seniors, rather than remaining deflated by the absence of younger people. If there is a solid nucleus of people with strong social-action commitments, the church might negotiate its way to make that its public posture and become a rallying place for people committed to social ministries. A small church cannot be all things to all people, but it can be a special place for a particular type of people.

A fundamental principle of the church growth movement is the acceptance and promotion of homogeneity. It is suggested that churches that grow are composed of like-minded people who seek like-minded people. What is being proposed here may look similar, but it is significantly different. The people in our church are far from clones, but they share a genuine commonness. An analogy can be drawn from architecture and college campuses. Some campuses are a hodgepodge of styles, sizes, periods, and placement, with no continuity, commonality, or coherence with the natural environment. Others are sterile, mass produced monuments to blandness which might have been lifted from a catalog of prefabricated structures. Churches should be neither. Part of their faithfulness and effectiveness comes from being harmonious with the surrounding setting, having enough in common that they can share a tradition, style, and vision, and having enough diversity that they share a variety of experience, gifts, and wisdom.

As suggested earlier, some churches will not grow *because* of their faithfulness. A decision to stay in a declining neighborhood rather than relocate in a growing suburb can result not in growth but in great faithfulness. A church may choose the Isaiah-like suffering servant role by adhering to an unpopular social stand and therefore be repellent to those seeking a comfortable pew. A church like Washington, D.C.'s Church of the Savior might faithfully choose to be a disciplined covenant community that people wanting a more permissive church experience will avoid.

An issue that our church is wrestling with is how to grow and still remain small. Even with a worshiping community of only sixty-five, we find it a challenge to ensure that everyone really knows everyone, that people do not feel superfluous, that all needs and concerns are heard and addressed, that structures and processes remain simple and responsive, and that we maintain a common identity and vision.

A wise church that does grow will spend as much time working at including as they do working at attracting. The attracting is frequently easier than the including. The most creative and perceptive people need to develop appropriate community-building strategies, such as name tags, church albums and biographies, planning processes, communications measures, eating and playing opportunities, study and spiritual-growth situations, evolving new traditions and rituals, and so on. A basic question to focus on is: How can we grow a "small" church?

If a small church overcomes its inferiority complex about its smallness, knows itself, cares about the Christian faith and the people present, is in a fertile field, and becomes a people offering a kind of experience and excitement people do not find elsewhere, it will grow. It must be recognized that potential members will quickly perceive in a church whether they are wanted merely to help keep a leaking ship afloat or whether they are being invited to join the crew of a ship that is on course and pursuing an important mission.

MORALE AND CONFLICT

There are many kinds of small churches. Some are sun-drenched, some are sunless, and some are variable, like the New England weather. Some are characterized by eternal optimism and some by terminal pessimism. Some have high morale and some have low morale. One can quickly feel where a church is on the morale continuum. Following are typical characteristics of high and low morale churches:

High Morale	Low Morale
Trust their environment	Feel under seige from outside
Believe they can pay their way	Fear of red ink
People are positive and optimistic	People are negative and pessimistic
Can point to successes	Recall mainly defeats
People feel cared about	People feel abused and forgotten
Commited to some mission	Little sense of commitment
Real, concerned leadership	Incompetent, uncaring leadership
Open to different ideas	Resist innovations
Enjoy being present	Attendance is a duty
Visitors are welcomed	Visitors are endured
Stress a theology of grace	Stress a theology of judgment
Faith is joyous	Faith is dutiful
People trust one another	People look for hidden motives
Physical atmosphere is warm and bright	Physical atmosphere cold and drab
Conflict happens but is handled	Conflict is cancerous
See promise in the future	Anticipate only a bleak future

Of course the above characteristics are interrelated. They feed on one another moving the tide one way or the other. A high-morale church needs to be aware of what accounts for its high morale and to work to maintain and deepen it. A low-morale or fragile-morale church can, with a core of conscientious people and wise leadership, develop and carry out strategies that can turn it in a positive direction. Many churches hesitate to take the most important initial step, which is to invite a competent resource person or consultant, to help them move in a new direction. They can look to their denomination, a neighboring church, a nearby seminary, a council of churches, or secular sources for such assistance.

The following twelve steps can lead to positive change.

1. Ask the people to pray for help in moving in a healthy direction.
2. Analyze the situation, getting information and opinions from a wide range of sources.
3. Identify some strengths and highlight them.
4. Take steps to make being together more pleasurable —for example, turn the heat up a couple of degrees, paint the walls, turn on the coffee and bring on the sweet rolls, ask for a shorter sermon.
5. Capitalize on the strengths—for example, if there is a nucleus of charming children, celebrate them, develop the Sunday school, bring them into part of the worship.
6. Get help in training the leadership to be more effective.
7. Plan some sure-fire successes; make sure they succeed; celebrate the success; do it again.
8. Identify and agree on the single, biggest problem; brainstorm every conceivable way of working at it; plan strategy and take responsibility for some progressive steps for either minimizing or resolving the problem; act; review what happened; start over.
9. Have a sermon series and Bible study series on the implications of Ephesians 1-4 for the particular situation.
10. Have the consultant or leader help resolve or manage one of the small or medium-sized conflicts, to help the members discover that conflict need not be injurious as well as to remove one thorn from the church's side.
11. Direct some energy beyond the church to a community need or mission project that most or all can agree on.

12. As a last resort, if subversive, destructive persons threaten to leave, accept their offer—with regrets.

Morale is critical to the quality of a church's life. High morale must be nourished; low morale can be turned around. Use of a half-dozen of the options on the above list will help. High morale has been the single most significant attribute of the Warwick church for a decade, and the results spinning off from that have been profound. And we still work hard to keep morale high.

Prevalent conflict lowers morale, and low morale makes conflict more prevalent and perilous. However, conflict is present in the happiest people, organizations, and churches. Charles A. Dailey of Dartmouth College wrote: "If no known conflict exists, one is probably mistaken [in thinking none exists]. Or perhaps there is too much complacency and not enough innovation."[18] Conflict is present in all churches, especially in small churches.

Small size is a factor. When there is a conflict between people or over an issue, it cannot be ignored, even if everyone is not involved or even if it is not a church issue. A few years ago seven of our people were involved in a conflict stemming largely from issues outside the church. With these seven temporarily absent or distracted from church life, 20 percent of our active, worshiping adults were absent or distracted. And even when only a few are involved, the atmosphere is heavy for everyone.

The small size also means that the whole congregation can be involved in working through a church conflict to a decision or an understanding. Everyone can be heard. People will generally want to hear from all the others. They can all know what is going on. It is easier to sort out rumor from fact. There have been several examples at our church of conflicts over issues that have been chewed over until we had a harmonious consensus decision.

Conflict in the rural or small-town small church is made more difficult by the convergence of community and church. In the small town and the small church, church and world cannot and should not be separated, but it certainly muddies

171

the waters. Virtually any community issue will have church people on both sides. And small-town issues that bear directly on people's lives are going to feel more intense to the participants than more global issues such as race, war, and politics.

There are several possible ways for a pastor and/or church to minister to conflicting persons or in conflict situations. Be an enabler of communication. In one situation I was the mutually agreed upon interpreter between town officials and an aggrieved person. Be a forum where issues and feelings can be aired, considered, and resolved or understood. Reestablish the old custom of sanctuary, where within the church building people were safe from attack. Encourage the conflicting parties to come and coexist in the same space, even when they feel very hostile. Be a leader in the search for alternatives, so that all parties can win all or part of what they want, rather than having just winners and losers. Allow people, when necessary, to retreat without being made to feel they are disloyal to the church. Be a channel of God's grace through whom, in worship and pastoral care, the Spirit of God can work reconciliation.

Carl Dudley is right—small churches are free to fight.

> They can afford to fight, because they are not held together by rational commitments, nor the outcome of any particular decision. The ties that hold most small churches are in the past: family and people, space and territory, history and tradition, culture carrying in the Christian faith. These are commitments of the heart. The pastor (or church members) who shares an appreciation of these elements can heal the most divided church and mobilize the most withdrawn congregation.[19]

PLANNING

Planning turns a few people on—and turns many off. Most churches, if honest, would admit they do not have any articulated goals for the whole church. Yet virtually every church has goals—to stay open, to have a Sunday school, to keep the minister, to get rid of the minister, to make the budget, to fill the pews, and so on.

There are many reasons goals are not written down in churches. The minister may prefer to do it his or her way. People may fear that specific goals would divide the congregation. Some might feel goal-setting is a Harvard Business School practice and does not belong in the church. A variation on this is that specific goals might constrain the moving of the Spirit in their midst. The comfortable and fearful may fear that goals would require change. The pessimistic and pragmatic may think goals could lead to failure ("If we have no goals, there are no goals to fall short of"). More often churches do not set goals because they don't get around to it. What tends to happen in Warwick is that individual committees set goals, but we often don't proceed to goals for the whole congregation.

Articulated goals are important to churches, especially small ones. First, with fewer people it should be easier to find goals the whole congregation can accept and participate in. Second, with fewer people it is easier to mobilize people to work at the goals. Third, it is important that energy not be wasted in random wandering. Goals are particularly important when a church is in transition (i.e., new minister, changing membership, or changing community), when there is a crisis, when there is a unique opportunity, or when there are new people to be included in the life of the church.

Lyle Schaller suggests that goals should meet three criteria which combine to form the acronym SAM. A goal should be Specific (a goal to be a better church does not mean anything). A goal should be Attainable (a goal to eliminate conflict in a church is unattainable and self-defeating). A goal should be Measurable (a goal to increase worship attendance makes no distinction between an increase of one or fifty).[20]

Planning need not be tedious. It can be as interesting as watching a jigsaw puzzle, quilt, or child take shape. The following six-step goal-action process is simple, practical, and can produce satisfying results.

1. What do we want and/or need? What does the gospel call us to be/do? This involves collecting data about the church and community, surveying ideas and attitudes

of the membership, dreaming, Bible study, and worship. List; determine priorities; make each goal specific, attainable, and measurable; decide which goal or how many goals to tackle.

2. How might we do it? Dream again, brainstorm (don't criticize any idea), encourage each to contribute. At this stage do not be constrained by what you think is realistic.

3. How will we do it? This is the time for strategic decisions. But the strategies should require some stretching on your part. Before leaving this step, know what, how, and when it will be done, and who will do it.

4. Do it! And celebrate it!

5. How did we do it (or not do it)? Evaluate. What could or should have been done differently? What resources were discovered? What did we do right and wrong? How do we feel about what we did? Take time to share the anecdotes and stories. What are the next steps?

6. Do it again, SAM (Specifically, Attainably, Measurably).

Two words of warning about goals: First, individuals, groups, and churches tend to establish goals only to correct problems or bad habits. This can be self-defeating. Who wants to focus time and energy only on faults and mistakes? Have as many goals that capitalize on strengths and opportunities as goals that seek to transform problem areas. Second, goals are often established and then quickly forgotten. Assign someone, other than the minister, who is persistent, reliable, and loving to be your "goals watchdog"—the person who continually holds before you what you said you were going to do.

OUTSIDE RELATIONSHIPS

Small churches do not live in a vacuum. All are part of a surrounding community. Most are in some kind of relationship with neighboring or nearby churches. Again, size affects the way they relate, or do not relate, to community, churches, and denomination.

174

The type and quality of relationship between church and community can vary widely. The conservative Baptist church in a nearby town has erected a high wall between itself and its community. A Protestant church in a Catholic community, or a Catholic church in a Protestant community, might have a wall built around it by the community. In rural communities there is often little or no separation between church and community. I worked in a rural Methodist church that had fifteen to twenty in worship and the whole community working on its fair. In an urban setting a church can be almost invisible to those around it.

In families, when one member changes significantly, other family members frequently have difficulty adjusting to that change. When a church becomes revitalized, the surrounding neighborhood may be confused, suspicious, or resentful. In our situation the confluence of a very active church and a very small town has resulted in resentments and misunderstandings. As these feelings became apparent, we escalated our efforts to demonstrate our desire to serve the town rather than run it.

Regularly we make contributions to the community which are purely in the interest of goodwill and community service. We offer free use of the building to all community groups. Our Christmas and Easter letter to the community invites people to return the enclosed offering envelope to our church or any other. We are in the process of turning some of our land into a community recreation area. As members are involved in community affairs and issues, we urge them to act and speak as Christian people and not as representatives or advocates of our church. We try to be very public and candid with the larger community about such things as our budget, activities, and purposes. The result of these efforts is much community support and a parish of five hundred, while our membership is less than seventy.

Relationships among churches vary tremendously. One of the common sins of the Christian church is the isolation, alienation, and competition that often exist among churches. Churches of all sizes are guilty of seducing one another's members. Small churches struggling to survive sometimes find this a tempting strategy. Hostile or suspicious smaller

175

churches might consider the fable of the ox and the colt who went to the spring to drink. There was plenty of room and water for each, but they proceeded to argue about who should drink first. As the argument turned into a fight, they noticed the vultures circling over them, waiting for the battle. They decided it was better for them to drink together.

Small churches especially need to develop creative and cooperative relationships with one another. Carefully thought out and conscientiously carried through, this is usually a better option than merger, federation, competition, or foolish independence. Many forms of sharing might occur: bulk buying, shared office equipment and space, sharing of curriculum and resources, joint youth groups and church schools, combined training events and retreats, programming that complements rather than duplicates, sharing clergy, supporting one another's fund raising, sharing building space, and so on. The result might be not only conservation of costs and resources but also a more fruitful ministry and mission growing out of the cross-fertilization. For churches, being "one in Christ [Gal. 3:28]" might better mean being brothers and sisters in the family of churches, rather than being clones or composites.

Most denominations have responded to small churches with studies, resources, and concern. Some of these efforts have been patronizing, ill-informed, and misdirected; others have been on-target and helpful. Denominational responses to their small churches—which are generally the majority of their churches—have tended to be cosmetic and symptomatic rather than substantive. And sometimes they have been too little too late.

To small churches within denominations I would say:

Speak up. You are a legitimate member of the Body of Christ. When you hurt or are in need, ask for assistance. When you have a victory, ask your denomination to celebrate with you.

Speak out. Your form of church has a unique perspective and experience. The larger church needs to know what you know about intimacy, making do on a subsistence income, the possibilities and problems of small groups, worship and education, caring and mission. But speak up without being apologetic, defensive, or antagonistic—you will be better heard.

Honor the covenant. In all denominations there are mutual responsibilities and privileges."Just as no man is an island," no church is an independent organ in the Body of Christ. Even if a small church is poor, it can participate in the larger work of the church. Even if leadership is scarce and needed in the local church, some of that leadership can be shared (and thereby trained) with such larger bodies as the association, district, or synod.

To denominations and denominational officials I would say:

Listen. The small church is a different species, and each one is different from the others. Even if you grew up in or served in a small church in your early ministry, that does not mean you sufficiently understand this type of church. In order to serve it and utilize it, you must listen, get acquainted, and walk in its shoes.

Adapt. Most denominational programs, resources, mandates, and recommendations are designed for the large-church model. Can the denomination (after listening) adapt, rather than expect the small church to do all the adapting? Different strategies, methods, materials, and expectations may be called for.

Don't patronize. Small churches are not baby or junior churches. They do not ask you to be especially nice. They ask you to adapt standards, not lower them. Rather than affirmative action, how about fair action?

Advocate. Since denominations are human institutions, power politics is a part of them. Small churches have, at best, a small share of the power. Denominational officials can be advocates of small churches with the clergy retirement systems, so pastors who choose small churches are not discriminated against or penalized at retirement time. They can be advocates with nominating committees, to see that the competent leadership from small churches get represented. They can be advocates with program agencies, to see that small-church needs and opportunities get addressed. They can be advocates with the seminaries, to spend at least as much effort educating men and women for small-church leadership as they now do in preparing everyone for large-church leadership. They can be advocates with the placement people, to develop alternative forms of pastoral situations (bi-vocational is one good example) and to see that pastors of small churches are not discriminated against when they compete with their sisters and brothers in larger churches for new positions. They can be advocates with those who control the purse strings, to be more creative and visionary in seeding or subsidizing work in small churches. Don't speak for us, but use your louder voice to speak with us.

Ministry is what we all do in Christ's name (worship, education, caring) in the church; Mission is all that we all do beyond the church; Maintenance is what we all do to make our ministry and mission faithful and effective.

FOR DISCUSSION

1. What are the primary maintenance issues for your church?

2. Is your building a plus or a minus to your ministry and mission?

3. Does your organization serve the people, or do the people serve the organization?

4. Where is your church on the morale scale?

5. What are the goals (stated or not) of your church?

CHAPTER 8

small-church ministry

The minister is the church—true or false?

The church is ministry—true or false?

Frequently it seems as if "true" is the answer to the first question. Often ministers do most of the work and are behind most of the decisions, and to many people they are the church personified. Biblically and theologically the answer to that question is "false." The answer to the second question is "true"—the church is ministry. Henri Nouwen writes, "No Christian is a Christian without being a minister."[1]

Paul writes to the Ephesus church and reminds them, "And his [Christ's] gifts were that some should be apostles, some prophets, some evangelists, some pastors and teachers, to *equip the saints for the work of ministry,* for building up the body of Christ [Eph. 4:11-12]." The "saints" are not the supergood, but simply the people who are the church. Each had gifts which were to be called forth, developed, and utilized in ministry. The Greek word for ministry was *diakonia* (deacon), which meant table waiter.[2] The closest English translation is "servant" or "server." *Diakonia* was a term applied to the whole church and not just the leader(s). The distinction that the minister is the server, and the laity are the served, is not legitimate.

The New Testament church did not distinguish between minister and laity. Laity comes from *laos* and means the whole people of God. The correct understanding would be to merge ministers and lay people into "all the people of God who serve." The "minister" then becomes part of the laity, and the whole laity are the ministers of the church. The writer of 1 Peter supports the biblical theme of mutual ministry by referring to all the people of the church as a "royal priesthood" (1 Pet. 2:9).

This makes theological sense, but it makes problems for the writer who needs to distinguish for clarity's sake between the ordained and unordained or between those the church employs for ministry and those who volunteer for ministry. In this chapter, I will refer to the clergy or clergyperson and the lay person or lay people (still not an adequate term).

This is one of many areas where the small church can help its larger cousins. In larger churches the distinction between clergy and lay people has been sharp. Anyone who is theologically trained, ordained, and receives a professional salary is a "minister"; those who have not received such training and who receive no salary for their work in the church are lay people and eligible to participate in worship on Laity Sunday. In small churches where the "minister" may not have a full seminary education, or works full-time at a secular job, or is a seminarian, or comes only on Sunday (the day-to-day work of the church being done by the resident members), the distinctions are not as sharp. In our small church I am a person first and a clergyperson second. In a larger church I would be seen by most as clergyperson first, and then as a regular human being. If the concern is quality control, maintaining standards, or knowing who to admit to the retirement system, sharp distinctions are nice. If the concern is faithfulness, service, and theological integrity the distinctions seem artificial, arbitrary, and discriminatory.

James Fenhagen, dean of the General Theological Seminary in New York City, writes, "The greatest single obstacle to the genuine renewal of the church is the lack of mutuality that exists between the clergy and the laity."[3] Galatians 3:28, with an insertion, says it nicely: "In Christ there is neither Jew nor Greek, there is neither slave nor free, there is neither male nor female [clergy nor lay person], for you are all one in Christ Jesus." This is not to suggest that ordination and academic training for ministry are not important, or that churches should not employ people with special training and experience. There are authentic churches who are lay led by people who volunteer their gifts and time. However, the transformation of the Warwick church occurred in large measure because the members chose to employ a theologically and ecclesiastically trained and ordained person to spend a large block of time leading and training them in ministry. Without some remuneration, I could not have given the needed time, and without the training I could not have been as effective. Because small churches generally are not as clergy-dominated, they have a unique opportunity to pioneer some new forms of ministry and clergy-lay relationships.

There are biblical titles, or offices, for the people who are responsible for the five basic tasks of the Christian church. As a clergyperson I carry all these titles. The people who accept leadership responsibility in the church, and all those who accept responsibility for being the church, the laity, also carry some of these titles:

Priest. This is the title of those who lead in worship; those who help the people praise, confess, receive forgiveness, hear the word of God, and respond to it. The priest is a medium through whom God is revealed and the catalyst who brings God and person together. The liturgist, preacher, organist, choir, greeters, even the flower arrangers are priests. The one (ordained or not) who visits in the hospital, sits by the deathbed, or hears a confession in the workplace, and mediates grace via a good word is a priest. It is presumptuous of clergy to hoard the title of priest for themselves. One of my callings is to be a priest to lay priests, who in turn are priests to me and others.

Rabbi. The rabbi is the teacher or educator, the one who helps others learn and live the word. There is some teaching in all aspects of my ministry, but there are many rabbis in our church. When the children model kingdom-like qualities for the adults, the children are the rabbis. When the adults model the gifts of the Spirit and share their experience in the faith and family, they are the rabbis. Without our rabbis we would be ignorant people. When we teach we are equipping the saints—all of us.

Pastor. The pastor is the shepherd, the one who performs the ministry of caring for the flock and the lost or rebellious sheep. A church where only the clergyperson is a pastor will have a flock of forlorn and straying sheep. Members of a small church can be particularly effective at pastoring one another. In our church this is a ministry shared specifically with the deacons and generally with all. Each who cares in Christ's name is a pastor.

Deacon. This is the ministry of serving, the ministry of mission. The deacons are responsible not only for being the waiters or servers of the Lord's Supper but also for taking bread to the hungry, healing to the sick, taking clothes to the naked, making visitations to the imprisoned, and seeking freedom for the oppressed. When the people leave the building, they all go as deacons.

Bishop. The bishops are those who take care of the maintenance of the church—the treasurer, clerk, trustees, moderator or president, janitor, secretary, clergy, conflict managers, and communicators. They are the ones who see that the homemaking and housekeeping are taken care of.

Another important office cuts across lines of ordination and ecclesiastical responsibility—that of *the prophet*. The prophet is any person with the gift of perceiving God's presence or imperative in the secular world, or the secular application of the sacred word. Numbered among the prophets in the church might be a four-year-old child, an outcast, an outspoken newcomer, a noisy student, a quiet pillar of strength, and the one who preaches. Without the offerings of the prophets, the ministries of a church are likely to miscarry.

182

The apostle Paul warns that if every member of the Body of Christ does not function as it is supposed to, the Body becomes handicapped. In the same way, if the priests, rabbis, pastors, deacons, bishops, and prophets do not all carry out their ministries, the church's ministry is truncated. As we look at each of these ministries, we see that none of them carries the label "clergy only"—although some would try to usurp the priestly, pastoral, prophetic, and bishopric ministries solely for clergy. This year when we installed our new church officers and committees we gave each person one or more of these titles in addition to the more traditional designations.

Lay people in small churches may be more practiced at these ministries than those in large churches. When the senior minister and minister of music are the priests, the minister of education is chief rabbi, the minister of pastoral care is the primary caretaker, the minister to the community is the head deacon, and the sexton, secretary, and appointed and employed others act as a team of bishops (under the senior minister who is both chief priest and archbishop), the lay people become spectators who watch the action and pick up the tab.

This is one way of recognizing that—although they may be short on training, terminology, and technique—small churches are usually long on experienced and committed lay ministers—because they have to be. If the church has a part-time or shared clergyperson, it must share the ministry or it will not get done. If the clergyperson is inexperienced, the lay people must teach her or him small-church ministry and assume much of it.

BUT WHAT ABOUT THE CLERGY?

There have always been competent and compassionate clergy serving in small churches. However, small churches have more often been the clergy proving ground, dumping ground, and pasture for clergy who have not made it, who cannot make it, or who are too tired to make it any more. What Edwin Earp wrote in 1914 of the rural church has long been true of all small churches:

> The church of today will not win back its lost rural domain, nor win new fields of rural conquest, by sending to this field, as is too frequently the case, superannuated preachers, unprepared novices, or flunkers in preparatory schools or theological seminaries, or those who couldn't hold a city appointment. It will win only when it places in this field men who know and love the open country.[4]

The life and potential that lay dormant within small churches will not be awakened until additional skilled, gifted, and motivated clergy see them as their calling and not as stepping-stones toward bigger and better things. There are at least three reasons small churches have not had a fair shot at the clergy who are in demand: seminaries, salaries, and status.

Seminaries. Seminaries are where clergy develop their career attitudes and set their life goals. Seminaries are staffed by "successful" ex-pastors from larger churches, and professors who have spent most of their careers in academia. Few of these have experienced small churches as places where vital Christianity can and does happen. They do not know that small-church leadership requires unique skills and a special style. Preaching, Christian education, administration, and music specialists who are brought in to teach the practicalities of church life are usually from the large urban and suburban churches. Students are taught to administrate, preach, educate, and counsel where the people are many and the resources abound. In the seminarian's mind the image that grows of where and what a successful, significant professional ministry is, is that of the medium-sized and large church. Earp made a similar point almost seventy years ago: "In fact, our whole educational system in college, theological seminary, and public school, has been suffering from 'urbanitis'; the city interest has swallowed up the country interest."[5]

But more and more seminarians are choosing to minister in small churches. Three years ago I read all the fieldwork résumés at a prominent Boston seminary and discovered that several students were specifically interested in small churches and in rural settings.

184

Salaries. The image of ministry is established and the seminarian thinks about paying off seminary bills and perhaps starting a family and establishing a home. Or, as is now frequently the case, the seminarian is older and already has family responsibilities. He or she looks around at what other "professionals," union, and tradespeople earn, and then looks at what churches can afford to pay. What is true in many small churches today was true at the turn of the century when Gill and Pinchot wrote, "The salary of the average country minister in Windsor and Tompkins counties is not a living wage."[6] Their study went on to show that clergy salaries were not keeping up with the increased cost of living. A recent study claims that in 1950 a congregation of 60 regularly attending persons could afford a full-time pastor but that it took 150 regulars in 1980 to do the same.[7] Only a heavily endowed or unusually affluent small church can afford what is considered an adequate full-time salary. Thus most clergy attractive enough to be in demand go where they can get what they want or need, and those who are left divide up the small-salary situations. However, some clergy are discovering there are ways to make a living in small-church settings.

Status. Who doesn't want to be a "success"? And what is success in the church in the 1980s? It is really not much different from what it was decades ago. In a popular 1947 novel, *The Bishop's Mantle,* the hero is described:

> At nine o'clock on a bright March morning a young man in his first thirties walked slowly along High Street. He was tall with the shoulders and waist of an athlete. . . . His clothes were distinctly well-tailored and he wore them with an easy nonchalance. A stranger interested enough to hazard a guess might have set him down as a handsome young lawyer, or a business man with his feet well set upon the ladder of success. They would have probably not have surmised that he was a clergyman coming to assume the duties of his first large parish.[8]

Is that image of success any different from now? Robert Lynn and James Fraser describe how it was very different in the eighteenth century:

Americans have not always valued the large church more than the small one. In fact, in the eighteenth century during those decades just before the Revolution, no absolute distinction was made between the large and the small church. New England Congregationalist ministers, for example, did not necessarily move from smaller to larger churches. In fact, they didn't move. A study of the graduates of Yale College from 1702 to 1775 shows that 79 percent of those who were ministers served one parish all their lives. . . . A mere 7 percent had more than two parishes. In those days, it seems, an individual was called by God to a lifelong commitment to the people of God. . . . The situation was precisely the reverse of today, that is, Congregational pastors of that time looked upon themselves as holding identical problems. There were no essential spiritual distinctions between the minister who labored in a small Connecticut hamlet and the pastor of the prominent church in New Haven or Boston.[9]

I remember a poignant experience with the status issue. After being in Warwick about three years (six years after seminary), I was on the staff of a national youth conference in Wisconsin. There were several clergy there I knew, each of whom had recently made a move up the ladder of ecclesiastical success. By the end of the second day I was asking myself what was wrong with me. Was I not playing the game because I feared the competition? Was I working half-time for peanuts because I could do no better? Was there something wrong with me because I found satisfaction and meaning in ministering with a few people in a place even Massachusetts people had never heard of? It took about four days for the depression to lift and for me to believe again that I was a competent minister doing good work where I wanted to do it.

Whether because of low status, inadequate salaries, or poor matches, the clergy turnover rate in small churches has been high. Many small churches have complained they cannot keep ministers long enough to know and trust them. This may be changing. In a survey of United Church of Christ small churches in Massachusetts, I discovered that 50 percent of the state's small churches with full-time ordained clergy had had their clergy for four or more years. Seventy percent of those churches with part-time ordained clergy, or where clergy were serving more than one church, who had been present four or more years. This suggests that clergy may be staying longer in small churches and that clergy who have solved the financial and job satisfaction bind by having more than one employer can afford to stay where they would like to stay.

There seem to be three kinds of relationships between churches and clergy—one-night stands, living together, and marriage. Small churches in particular have been tantalized and plagued by a succession of one-night stands with a variety of clergy. A succession of seminary students, lay preachers, interims, experimenting seminary graduates, Bible school products, and various others would come, raise expectations, preach the same pitches that had been heard before, add a little life, and move on. Each time the congregation becomes more convinced that they don't deserve a lasting relationship and more certain no one wants such a relationship with them. Each time the church's reputation as "one of those churches" becomes more firmly established. The members become resigned and jaded in the belief that this is all that life has in store for them.

There are some luckier churches and clergy who find one another, become lovers, and live together. Each finds a little security in the other. They share times of euphoria and times of contentment. But since each suspects the intentions of the other, there are times of suspicion, resentment, and withdrawal. They become bored with each other. Sooner or later one feels used or sees a more enticing option and the arrangement is broken. Each tends to move on to a similar arrangement with a new partner. Most clergy and church relationships are of the lover/living together variety.

Then there are the creative, courageous churches and clergy who buck the prevailing trends and marry. In these relationships each party makes a commitment "to have and to hold from this day forward, for better or for worse, for richer or for poorer, in sickness and in health, to love and to honor." Each partner trusts the other, cares deeply about the other, and lives a separate life, but they grow together.

187

They nurture their children and watch them grow. They are proud of each other's strengths and accept (or endure) each other's idiosyncrasies. Because of the commitment they have made, they each run the risk of being jilted, but they take the risk anyway. Rather than each time being the same people or churches with different partners, they strive to grow and mature so that the relationship remains fresh and fertile. Sometimes, despite the greatest effort, they grow in different directions. When the marriage has been good and satisfying the parting is thankful and painful, and each wishes good for the other. My relationship with the Warwick church is a changing, growing marriage.

Small churches are very capable of forming marriages with a well-matched clergyperson. Why? In part because the numbers make it easier. Each of us has many aspects to our personality. Each person in a church is an aspect of that church's personality. The more aspects, the more complex the personality, and the more complex the personality, the more difficult the maintenance of a marriage. Small churches and their clergyperson can know each other better. This familiarity will breed either contempt or intimacy and empathy. Small churches will feel gratitude to the clergyperson who respects and loves them. The clergyperson will know that although she or he is not touching great numbers of lives, a few lives are being greatly touched.

As with most marriages, one of the greatest problems for the small church-clergy marriage is how they are each going to make ends meet. While doing pastoral counseling, I have learned that financial difficulty is one of the greatest causes of marital stress. The same is true for clergy and churches. The church feels hard-pressed and gets discouraged or desperate as it tries to be fair with the clergy. He or she grows resentful and feels shortchanged when state or national clergy salary averages are published. What can be done?

Yoking two or more churches, federations of churches, and denominational subsidies are three options frequently chosen. Each has virtues, but also serious drawbacks. Yoked and federated situations often feel polygamous. Jealousies about time, money, housing, and programs often abound.

Subsidized churches feel as if they are living off the in-laws, and the in-laws feel as if they have a right to interfere.

The alternative that has worked well for us and many others is the bi-vocational model of ministry. A National Council of Churches Clergy Support Study conducted in 1974 revealed that 22 percent of the clergy in major denominations are in the bi-vocational, or tentmaker, category. This 22 percent was divided into two groups: part-timers (13 percent), who are in secular jobs twenty to forty hours a week; and moonlighters (9 percent), who receive nonchurch income for one to twenty hours of work.[10] Worker priest, self-supporting minister, nonstipendiary clergyperson, minister-worker, and dual-role minister are some of the other terms used to describe this kind of ministry. With present economic trends and an oversupply of clergy in some regions, that 22 percent will grow into one third or even one half of all clergy.

It would be a mistake to believe this is a second-class ministry or one whose only virtue is a livable total salary. Bi-vocational ministry was the norm for the first three or four hundred years of the Christian church. "It has served well to meet the needs of Paul at Philippi, the monks in medieval cloisters, the Reformers adrift from traditional controls and financial stability, the pioneer families on the frontier plains, or struggling congregations on the crossroads of twentieth-century America."[11]

A bi-vocational ministry has several virtues. Instead of having to share a clergyperson with another church, the church has "our own minister." The clergyperson experiences the real world where the lay people work and minister, which results in his or her church ministry being more relevant to them in their particular situations. It provides the clergyperson with an arena for ministry in a secular setting which would otherwise be off limits. Whether the clergyperson is driving a bus or teaching college classes, the combination can result in a cross-fertilization that keeps him or her fresh, informed, and creative. It forces one to decide what is most important in the ministry to and through the church. Since everything cannot be done, the most important areas can be focused on. Lay people have to assume some of the responsibilities that full-time clergy often end up doing. And a bi-vocational ministry helps keep finances from reaching the crisis point for both church and clergy.

On a personal level, bi-vocational ministry has brought great variety and challenge to my life. While fatigue is part of that life, boredom never is. Because one of my jobs is being a househusband while my wife is teaching, I have been able to spend precious time with my children—to their benefit and mine. My schedule is my own and is respected by the church. Never has anyone complained about being short-changed. The essentials are taken care of, and the church functions just as well with fewer meetings, fewer mailings, and fewer administrative maneuvers. While my whole life is ministry, I am better at it and for it by doing it professionally only part-time. I have no desire to serve a church full-time. For me this has been the best of two worlds.

Bi-vocational ministry is not a panacea, however. The clergyperson is not always going to be available when people want him or her. There is frequently not enough time to be divided between church, job, family, and self. Denominations sometimes do not know what to do with bi-vocationals when it comes to things like retirement programs and insurance. There are examples of bi-vocational arrangements in which the clergyperson gives the secular job priority and the church becomes the odd job. A present problem is that seminaries, denominations, and churches seldom think about or know how to establish a bi-vocational situation. Usually it is the clergyperson who forges the way.[12]

The Christian church would be well served if the whole church establishment would recognize that bi-vocational ministry is a legitimate style of ministry, present it as a necessary, viable option, and make it possible for clergy in certain situations. Seminaries should emphasize the biblical, theological, and historical rationale for this style of ministry and help interested students inventory their experience, gifts, and skills to determine what employment alternatives are appropriate for them.

Denominational staff could explore with appropriate congregations the benefits and liabilities of a bi-vocational ministry for that setting. The church could be helped to survey the range of job options in its area. Sometimes a congregation could tailor a bi-vocational combination. For example, a local industry might be interested in an industrial chaplaincy. A joint search committee (representing both the church and the industry) might meet with candidates to identify the one who is best for both. Denominations need to make adjustments to give bi-vocational ministry the place and the integrity it deserves. For example, the UCC *Manual on the Ministry* does not even recognize this form of ministry.

The small church cannot compete with larger churches in the salary it can pay or the status it can bestow, but it can compete in the amount of care it can give, the opportunity to be needed, and the willingness to let the clergyperson be real and a member of the family. To choose to minister in a small church is more than to accept a call, it is to choose a special style of life. For me this special lifestyle has been challenging and rewarding, captivating and freeing. Like everything else about a small church, ministry there is different. For some it is as comfortable as an old shoe, and for others it can be as constricting as a new girdle. Homemakers will be happier than housekeepers. Those who understand what the Shakers meant by "It is a gift to be simple" will belong. Small-church people are not as impressed with degrees, vestments, and a professional aura as they are by approachability, availability, and reliability. Not only do they look for these qualities, but they offer them to those they trust.

Small churches should be clear about what they offer and what they do not, and about what they need and do not need in a clergyperson. Not everyone is suited for ministry in a small church. Clergy who make the best small-church ministers are:

• People who would rather be themselves than project an image

- People whose own sense of worth can withstand anonymity and who can give worth to others and see worth in all
- People who appreciate the potential of a tiny mustard seed or a bit of yeast
- People creative enough to make a silk purse out of a sow's ear and practical enough to make good use of a silk purse
- People who have the sensitivity to ignore the pressing crowd so they can feel the touch of the hemorrhaging woman or see little Zacchaeus in the sycamore tree
- People who know God calls the church to be faithful and effective, not big and successful
- People who have the special skills of the general practitioner

FOR DISCUSSION

1. How would your church define ministry?

2. Do your lay people tend to see their daily living as ministry? Do you?

3. How much clergy does your church need? Full-time? Part-time?

4. What kinds of relationships has your church had with recent clergy?

5. What do you want from your clergy? What do you give your clergy?

CONCLUSION

"It has become part of the American character not only to accept bigness but actually to admire, respect, love, at times even worship bigness. Size is the measure of excellence: in cars, tomatoes, cigarettes, houses, breasts, audiences, salaries, freeways, skyscrapers, muscles. . . ."[1] I have tried to demonstrate and illustrate that small churches, as part of a bigger-is-better world, are the right size to do everything God wants of a church. The things they are not the right size for are contemporary accretions and not part of the biblical, historical, and theological charter. If a church grows, it does not necessarily become better, just bigger. Size is not God's criteria of faithfulness.

The second theme of this book has been that small is different. The size of a church will determine not only what happens but how it happens. Small churches will and should do things differently, not because they are obstinate or peculiar but simply because they are small. Their worship, learning, serving, caring, maintaining, and ministering will look, feel, sound, smell, and taste different.

As I have labored intensely on this book, and as I have looked at groups and churches from the small-church perspective, these two themes appear to me to be both obvious and critically important. It is important that the residents of small churches affirm and capitalize on the power and potential of their God-given size. And it is essential that servants of these churches help them fulfill what they are and not try to make them what they are not.

Now remember what you were . . . when God called you. From the human point of view few of you were wise or powerful or of high social standing. God purposefully chose what the world considers nonsense in order to shame the wise, and he chose what the world considers weak in order to shame the powerful. He chose what the world looks down on and despises and thinks is nothing, in order to destroy what the world thinks is important. . . . By him we are put right with God; and we become God's holy people and are set free.

—1 Corinthians 1:26-30, NEB

Small churches are indeed the right size!

NOTES

Introduction

1. Loren B. Mead, Preface to *Unique Dynamics of the Small Church* by Carl S. Dudley (Washington, DC: Alban Institute, 1977).
2. James L. Lowery Jr., "The Small Church Is Here to Stay and She Can Be Viable" (Paper prepared for the Annual Meeting of the Religious Research Association, Boston, 1974), p. 2.
3. Ibid., pp. 4-5 (italics added).
4. Carl S. Dudley, *Making the Small Church Effective* (Nashville: Abingdon Press, 1978), p. 24. Used by permission.
5. Ibid., p. 21. Used by permission.
6. Ibid., p. 35. Used by permission.

Chapter 1: A Dream Come True

1. Charles A. Morse, "The Story of the Congregational Church of Warwick, Massachusetts" (1969), p. 22.
2. Ibid., p. 34.
3. Ibid., p. 30.
4. Carl Sandburg, "Washington Monument by Night," in *Chief Modern Poets of England and America,* ed. Gerald Dewitt Sanders, et al. (New York: Macmillan, 1962), vol. 2, p. 126.
5. John E. Skoglund, *Worship in the Free Churches* (Valley Forge, PA: Judson Press, 1965), pp. 133-35.
6. Morse, "The Story of the Congregational Church," p. 37.
7. H. Richard Niebuhr, *The Purpose of the Church and Its Ministry* (New York: Harper & Row, 1956), pp. 79-94.
8. "Minister, Church Accepted for Seminary," *Athol* (MA) *Daily News,* January 21, 1977, p. 3.

Chapter 2: What Is a Small Church?

1. Carl S. Dudley, *Making the Small Church Effective* (Nashville: Abingdon Press, 1978), p. 23. Used by permission.
2. Kirkpatrick Sale, *Human Scale* (New York: Coward, McCann & Geoghegan, 1980), p. 181.
3. Dudley, *Making the Small Church Effective,* p. 22.

4. E.F. Schumacher, *Small Is Beautiful* (New York: Harper & Row, Harper Colophon Books, 1973), p. 63.
5. Winthrop S. Hudson, *Religion in America* (New York: Charles Scribner's Sons, 1965), p. 411.
6. Richard G. Hutcheson Jr., "Pluralism and Consensus: Why Mainline Church Mission Budgets Are in Trouble," *The Christian Century*, July 6-13, 1977, p. 620.
7. Paul O. Madsen, *The Small Church—Valid, Vital, Victorious* (Valley Forge, PA: Judson Press, 1975), pp. 111-12.
8. *Grassroots*, no. 2 (Winter 1978), p. 7.
9. Schumacher, *Small Is Beautiful*, p. 62.
10. Hudson, *Religion in America*, pp. 375-76.
11. Lyle E. Schaller, "Looking at the Small Church: A Frame of Reference," *The Christian Ministry*, July 1977, pp. 5-6.
12. Jackson W. Carroll, ed., *Small Churches Are Beautiful* (New York: Harper & Row, 1977), p. x.
13. Schaller, "Looking at the Small Church," p. 5.
14. James L. Lowery Jr., "The Small Church Is Here to Stay and She Can Be Viable" (Paper prepared for the Annual Meeting of the Religious Research Association, Boston, 1974), p. 2.
15. Schaller, "Looking at the Small Church," p. 5.
16. Dudley, *Making the Small Church Effective*, p. 35. Used by permission.
17. Rockwell C. Smith, *Rural Ministry and the Changing Community* (Nashville: Abingdon Press, 1971), p. 16.
18. Douglas A. Walrath, "Types of Small Congregations and Their Implications for Planning," in *Small Churches Are Beautiful*, pp. 34-60.
19. Ibid., pp. 44-46.
20. Madsen, *The Small Church*, pp. 19-26.
21. Sale, *Human Scale*, p. 60.
22. Amos H. Hawley, *Human Ecology* (New York: Ronald Press, 1950), p. 122.
23. A. Paul Hare, *Handbook of Small Group Research* (New York: Free Press, 1962), p. 21.
24. Carl S. Dudley, "Membership Growth: The Impossible Necessity," *The Christian Ministry*, July 1977, p. 9.
25. Charles Horton Cooley, *Social Organization* (New York: Charles Scribner's Sons, 1929), p. 33.
26. Ibid., p. 92.
27. Kurt H. Wolff, *The Sociology of Georg Simmel* (New York: Free Press, 1950), p. 89.
28. Carl S. Dudley, "Small Churches Are Special," *JED Share*, Spring 1979, p. 5.
29. Carl S. Dudley, *Unique Dynamics of the Small Church* (Washington, DC: Alban Institute, 1977), pp. 20-21.
30. Edwin L. Earp, *The Rural Church Movement* (New York: Methodist Book Concern, 1914), p. 166.

31. Samuel W. Blizzard, "The Roles of the Rural Parish Minister, the Protestant Seminaries, and the Sciences of Social Behavior," *The Sociology of Religion: An Anthology,* ed. Richard D. Knudten (New York: Appleton-Century-Crofts, 1967), p. 246.
32. Walter L. Cook, *Send Us a Minister . . . Any Minister Will Do* (Rockland, ME: Courier-Gazette, 1978), p. 151.

Chapter 3: Worship: The Family Reunion of the Body of Christ

1. Miriam Therese Winter, *Preparing the Way of the Lord* (Nashville: Abingdon Press, 1978), p. 49. Used by permission.
2. Edward Schweizer, *Church Order in the New Testament* (London: SCM Press, 1959), p. 186.
3. William H. Willimon and Robert L. Wilson, *Preaching and Worship in the Small Church* (Nashville: Abingdon Press, 1980), pp. 65-66.
4. Evelyn Underhill, *Worship* (New York: Harper & Row, 1937), p. 3.
5. James F. White, *The Worldliness of Worship* (New York: Oxford University Press, 1967), p. 20.
6. Henri J.M. Nouwen, *Creative Ministry* (New York: Image Books, 1978), p. 37.
7. There are good chapters on the locale of worship in John E. Skoglund's *Worship in the Free Church* (Valley Forge, PA: Judson Press, 1965), pp. 109-35; in James F. White's *New Forms of Worship* (Nashville: Abingdon Press, 1971), pp. 80-99; and in Rey O'Day and Edward A. Powers' *Theatre of the Spirit* (New York: The Pilgrim Press, 1980), pp. 70-86.
8. Gilbert Cope, ed., *Making the Building Serve the Liturgy* (London: A.R. Mowbray, 1962), p. 5.
9. Winter, *Preparing the Way of the Lord,* p. 78. Used by permission.
10. Ibid., pp. 80-81.
11. Dietrich Bonhoeffer, *Life Together,* trans. John W. Doberstein (New York: Harper & Row, 1954), pp. 60-61 (emphasis added).
12. Paul Tillich, "You Are Accepted," *The Shaking of the Foundations* (New York: Charles Scribner's Sons, 1948), pp. 153-63.
13. O'Day and Powers, *Theatre of the Spirit,* p. 19.
14. John Westerhoff III, *Bringing Up Children in the Christian Faith* (Minneapolis: Winston Press, 1980).
15. Anthony Trollope, *Barchester Towers and The Warden* (New York: Random House, Modern Library, 1950), p. 252.
16. Nouwen, *Creative Ministry,* pp. 35-39.
17. Ibid., p. 40.
18. Bonhoeffer, *Life Together,* p. 122.
19. Willimon and Wilson, *Preaching and Worship in the Small Church,* p. 69.

Chapter 4: Education: Can Anything Good Grow in Nazareth?

1. Warren J. Hartman, from the 1978 report of the Department of Statistics, Council on Finance and Administration, The United Methodist Church, Nashville.
2. From *Will Our Children Have Faith?* by John H. Westerhoff III (New York: Seabury Press, 1976), p. 11. Copyright © 1976 by The Seabury Press, Inc. Used by permission of the publisher.
3. Ibid., p. 82. Used by permission of the publisher.
4. Ibid., p. 84. Used by permission of the publisher.
5. Frances W. Eastman, ed., *Guidelines for Evaluating Christian Education in the Local Church* (New York: United Church Press, 1973), p. 16.
6. Helpful resources on the learning center approach can be found in the following: *Learning in the Small Church,* a packet of six booklets, which can be ordered from the General Assembly Mission Board, Presbyterian Church in the U.S., 341 Ponce de Leon Avenue, N.E., Atlanta, Georgia 30365; Joan Edgerton, *Learning Centers* (Atlanta: John Knox Press, 1976); and Phyllis C. White, *The Broadly Graded Group: A Manual for Children in the Church* (Memphis: Board of Christian Education, Cumberland Presbyterian Church, 1981).
7. David Ray, "Can Anything Good Come from Nazareth?" in *Explore,* ed. Barbara Middleton (Valley Forge, PA: Judson Press, 1978), vol. 3, p. 111.
8. Donald L. Griggs, *Teaching Teachers to Teach: A Basic Manual for Church Teachers* (Nashville: Abingdon Press, 1980).

Chapter 5: Mission: Not Station to Station but Person to Person

1. Richard G. Hutcheson Jr., "Pluralism and Consensus: Why Mainline Church Mission Budgets Are in Trouble," *The Christion Century,* July 6-13, 1977, pp. 619-21.
2. Carl S. Dudley, *Unique Dynamics of the Small Church* (Washington, DC: Alban Institute, 1977), p. 6.
3. Ibid., p. 11.
4. Ibid., p. 12.
5. Carl S. Dudley, *Making the Small Church Effective* (Nashville: Abingdon Press, 1978), pp. 47-48.
6. Paul O. Madsen, *The Small Church—Valid, Vital, Victorious* (Valley Forge, PA: Judson Press, 1975), pp. 61-62.
7. Edwin L. Earp, *the Rural Church Movement* (New York: Methodist Book Concern, 1914), p. 88.
8. Orlando E. Costas, *The Integrity of Mission* (New York: Harper & Row, 1979), p. 91.
9. Hendrik Kraemer, *A Theology of the Laity* (Philadelphia: Westminster Press, 1958), pp. 99-100.

10. Arthur Simon, *Bread for the World* (New York: Paulist Press, 1975), p. 13.
11. Two other helpful mission planning tools are: Henry A. Blunk, *Small Church Mission Study Guide* (Philadelphia: Geneva Press, 1978); and George Brown Jr., *Mission, A Congregational Life/Intergenerational Experience* (New York: United Church Press, 1978).
12. Philip Hallie, *Lest Innocent Blood Be Shed* (New York: Harper & Row, 1979), p. 57.

Chapter 6: Caring: A Genius for Growing Real People

1. Margery Williams, *The Velveteen Rabbit* (New York: Avon Books, 1975), pp. 16-32. Used by permission of the original publisher, William Heinemann Ltd.
2. Howard J. Clinebell Jr., *The Mental Health Ministry of the Local Church* (Nashville: Abingdon Press, 1965), Introduction.
3. Elizabeth O'Connor, *Eighth Day of Creation* (Waco, TX: Word Books, 1971), p. 13.
4. See Abraham H. Maslow, "A Theory of Human Motivation," *Psychological Review* 50 (1943): 370-96.
5. Carl S. Dudley, *Making the Small Church Effective* (Nashville: Abingdon Press, 1978), p. 48. Used by permission.
6. Dietrich Bonhoeffer, *Life Together,* trans. John W. Doberstein (New York: Harper & Row, 1954), p. 94.
7. O'Connor, *Eighth Day of Creation,* p. 17.
8. Henri J.M. Nouwen, *Reaching Out* (Garden City, NY: Doubleday, 1975), p.46.
9. Gabriel Moran, "Community and Family: The Way We Are: Communal Forms and Church Response," in *Parish Religious Education,* ed. Maria Harris (New York: Paulist Press, 1978), p. 29.
10. Elizabeth O'Connor, *The New Community* (New York: Harper & Row, 1976), p. 58.
11. Henri J.M. Nouwen, *The Wounded Healer* (Garden City, NY: Doubleday, 1972), p. 94.
12. Ibid., p. 95.
13. James C. Fenhagen, *Mutual Ministry* (New York: Harper & Row, 1976), p. 9.
14. O'Connor, *The New Community,* p. 9.
15. Bruno Bettelheim, *A Home for the Heart* (New York: Knopf, 1974), p. 307.
16. Speed Leas and Paul Kittlaus, *Church Fights* (Philadelphia: Westminster Press, 1973), p. 43.
17. Dean R. Hoge and David A. Roozen, eds., *Understanding Church Growth and Decline: 1950–1978* (New York: Pilgrim Press, 1979), p. 64.

Chapter 7: Maintenance: Homemaking or Housekeeping

1. Paul O. Madsen, *The Small Church—Valid, Vital, Victorious* (Valley Forge, PA: Judson Press, 1975), pp. 10, 16.
2. Carl S. Dudley, *Making the Small Church Effective* (Nashville: Abingdon Press, 1978), pp. 71-74.
3. Virginia Satir, *Peoplemaking* (Palo Alto, CA: Science and Behavior Books, 1972), p. 282.
4. Madsen, *The Small Church*, p. 50.
5. Walter L. Cook, *Send Us a Minister . . . Any Minister Will Do* (Rockland, ME: Courier-Gazette, 1978), p. 81.
6. *The Avery and Marsh Songbook* (Port Jervis, NY: Proclamation Productions, 1972), p. 32. Used by permission.
7. Godfrey Sperling Jr., "Reflections from Fritz" in "Washington Letter," *Christian Science Monitor,* December 29, 1980, p. 8. Reprinted by permission from *The Christian Science Monitor.* © 1980 The Christian Science Publishing Society. All rights reserved.
8. Kurt H. Wolff, *The Sociology of Georg Simmel* (New York: Free Press, 1950), p. 87.
9. *Church Planning: A Manual for Use in the United Church of Christ* (New York: United Church of Christ Office for Church Life and Leadership, 1976), pp. C4-C5.
10. Ibid., pp. C1-C2.
11. Kenyon L. Butterfield, *The Country Church and the Rural Problem* (Chicago: University of Chicago Press, 1911), p. 125. The book was the publication of Butterfield's Carew Lectures at Hartford Seminary in 1909.
12. Alan K. Waltz, "Organizational Structures for the Small Congregation," in *Small Churches Are Beautiful,* ed. Jackson W. Carroll (New York: Harper & Row, 1977), pp. 150-51.
13. Ibid., p. 152.
14. Douglas A. Walrath, "Types of Small Congregations and Their Implications for Planning," in *Small Churches Are Beautiful,* pp. 33-60.
15. James L. Lowery Jr., "The Small Church Is Here to Stay and She Can Be Viable (Paper prepared for the Annual Meeting of the Religious Research Association, Boston, 1974), p. 2.
16. Madsen, *The Small Church*, p. 40.
17. Dudley, *Making the Small Church Effective*, p. 116. Used by permission.
18. Charles A. Dailey, "The Management of Conflict," *Chicago Theological Seminary Register,* May 1969, p. 7.
19. Carl S. Dudley, *Unique Dynamics of the Small Church* (Washington, DC: Alban Institute, 1977), p. 20.
20. Schaller, *Survival Tactics in the Parish*, p. 157.

Chapter 8: Small-church Ministry

1. Henri J.M. Nouwen, *Creative Ministry* (Garden City, NY: Doubleday, 1978), p. 114.
2. Hendrik Kraemer, A Theology of the Laity (Philadelphia: Westminster Press, 1958), p. 138.
3. James C. Fenhagen, *Mutual Ministry* (New York: Seabury Press, 1977), p. 23.
4. Edwin L. Earp, *The Rural Church Movement* (New York: Methodist Book Concern, 1914), p. 36.
5. Ibid., p. 165.
6. Charles Otis Gill and Gifford Pinchot, *The Country Church* (New York: Macmillan 1913), p. 49.
7. John Y. Elliott, *Our Pastor Has an Outside Job* (Valley Forge, PA: Judson Press, 1980), p. 6.
8. Agnes Sigh Turnbull, *The Bishop's Mantle* (New York: Macmillan, 1947), quoted in Robert W. Lynn and James W. Fraser, "Images of the Small Church in American History," in *Small Churches Are Beautiful*, ed. Jackson W. Carroll (New York: Harper & Row, 1977), p. 6.
9. Ibid., pp. 6-7.
10. James L. Lowery Jr., ed., *Case Histories of Tentmakers* (Wilton, CT: Morehouse-Barlow Co., 1976), p. 77.
11. Elliott, *Our Pastor Has an Outside Job*, p. 20.
12. John Elliott's *Our Pastor Has an Outside Job* is a report on the CODE project (Clergy Occupational Development and Employment project) in western New York. It offers guidelines and checklists for clergy, churches, and denominations that are interested in pursuing this style of ministry.

Conclusion

1. Kirkpatrick Sale, *Human Scale* (New York: Coward, McCann & Geoghegan, 1980), p. 64.

SELECTED BIBLIOGRAPHY

Books

Bettelheim, Bruno. *A Home for the Heart.* New York: Knopf, 1974.

Blizzard, Samuel W. "The Roles of the Rural Parish Minister, the Protestant Seminaries, and the Sciences of Social Behavior." In *The Sociology of Religion: An Anthology.* Edited by Richard D. Knudten. New York: Appleton-Century-Crofts, 1967.

Blunk, Henry A. *Smaller Church Mission Guide.* Philadelphia: Geneva Press, 1978.

Bonhoeffer, Dietrich. *Life Together.* Translated by John W. Doberstein. New York: Harper & Row, 1954.

Brown, George Jr. *Mission: A Congregational Life/Intergenerational Experience.* New York: United Church Press, 1978.

Butterfield, Kenyon L. *The Country Church and the Rural Problem.* Chicago: University of Chicago Press, 1911.

Carroll, Jackson W., ed. *Small Churches are Beautiful.* San Francisco: Harper & Row, 1977.

Church Planning: A Manual for Use in the United Church of Christ. Produced by the Office for Church Life and Leadership, 1976.

Clinebell, Howard J. Jr. *Basic Types of Pastoral Counseling.* Nashville: Abingdon Press, 1966.

————. *The Mental Health Ministry of the Local Church.* Nashville: Abingdon Press, 1965.

Cook, Walter L. *Send Us a Minister . . . Any Minister Will Do.* Rockland, ME: Courier-Gazette, 1978.

Cooley, Charles Horton. *Social Organization.* New York: Charles Scribner's Sons, 1929.

Cope, Gilbert, ed. *Making the Building Serve the Liturgy.* London: A.R. Mowbray, 1962.

Costas, Orlando E. *The Integrity of Mission.* New York: Harper & Row, 1979.

Dudley, Carl S. *Making the Small Church Effective.* Nashville: Abingdon Press, 1978.

————. *Where Have All Our People Gone?* New York: Pilgrim Press, 1979.

Duncan, Dudley Otis, and Reiss, Albert J. Jr. *Social Characteristics of Urban and Rural Communities.* New York: John Wiley & Sons, 1956.

Earp, Edwin L. *The Rural Church Movement.* New York: Methodist Book Concern, 1914.

Eastman, Frances W. *Guidlines for Evaluating Christian Education in the Local Church.* New York: United Church Press, 1973.

Elliott, John Y. *Our Pastor Has an Outside Job.* Valley Forge, PA: Judson Press, 1980.

Fenhagen, James C. *Mutual Ministry.* New York: Harper & Row, 1976.

Gill, Charles Otis, and Pinchot, Gifford. *The Country Church.* New York: Macmillan, 1913.

Gore, William J., and Hodapp, Leroy C., eds. *Change in the Small Community.* New York: Friendship Press, 1976.

Hallie, Philip. *Lest Innocent Blood Be Shed.* New York: Harper & Row, 1979.

Hare, A. Paul. *Handbook of Small Group Research.* New York: Free Press, 1962.

Hawley, Amos H. *Human Ecology.* New York: Ronald Press, 1950.

Henrichsen, Margaret. *Seven Steeples.* Boston: Houghton Mifflin Co., 1953.

Hoge, Dean R., and Roozen, David A., eds. Understanding Church Growth and Decline: 1950-1978. New York: Pilgrim Press 1979.

Hudson, Winthrop S. *Religion in America.* New York: Charles Scribner's Sons, 1965.

Kraemer, Hendrik. *A Theology of the Laity.* Philadelphia: Westminster Press, 1958.

Learning in the Small Church. Atlanta: John Knox Press, 1976.

Leas, Speed, and Kittlaus, Paul. *Church Fights.* Philadelphia: Westminster Press, 1973.

Lowery, James L. Jr., ed. *Case Histories of Tentmakers.* Wilton, CT: Morehouse-Barlow Co., 1976.

Madsen, Paul O. *Small Churches—Vital, Valid, Victorious.* Valley Forge, PA: Judson Press, 1975.

Maslow, Abraham H. "A Theory of Human Motivation," *Psychological Review* 50 (1943): 370-96.

Meek, Pauline Palmer. *Ministries with Children in Small Churches.* Philadelphia: Geneva Press, 1975.

Mitchell, Robert H. *Ministry and Music.* Philadelphia: Westminster Press, 1978.

Moran, Gabriel. "Community and Family: The Way We Are: Communal Forms and Church Response." In *Parish Religious Education,* pp. 25-40. Edited by Maria Harris. New York: Paulist Press, 1978.

Niebuhr, H. Richard. *The Purpose of the Church and Its Ministry.* New York: Harper & Row, 1956.

Nouwen, Henri J.M. *Creative Ministry.* Garden City, NY: Doubleday, 1971; Image Books, 1978.

————. *Reaching Out.* Garden City, NY: Doubleday, 1975.

————. *The Wounded Healer.* Garden City, NY: Doubleday, 1972.

O'Connor, Elizabeth. *Eighth Day of Creation.* Waco, TX: Word Books, 1971.

————. *The New Community.* New York: Harper & Row, 1976.

Olmstead, Michael S. *The Small Group.* New York: Random House, 1959.

Plunkett, Sir Horace. *The Rural Life Problem in the United States.* New York: Macmillan, 1910.

Ray, David. "Can Anything Good Come from Nazareth?" In *Explore,* vol. 3, pp. 109-12. Edited by Barbara Middleton. Valley Forge, PA: Judson Press, 1978.

Sale, Kirkpatrick. *Human Scale.* New York: Coward, McCann & Geoghegan, 1980.

Satir, Virginia. *Peoplemaking.* Palo Alto, CA: Science and Behavior Books, 1972.

Schaller, Lyle E. *Survival Tactics in the Parish.* Nashville: Abingdon Press, 1977.

Schumacher, E.F. *Small Is Beautiful.* New York: Harper & Row, 1973; Harper Colophon Books, 1975.

Schweizer, Edward. *Church Order in the New Testament.* London: SCM Press, 1959.

Skoglund, John E. *Worship in the Free Churches.* Valley Forge, PA: Judson Press, 1965.

Smith, Rockwell D. *Rural Ministry and the Changing Community.* Nashville: Abingdon Press, 1971.

Thompson, Bard, ed. *Liturgies of the Western Church.* Cleveland: World Publishing Co., 1961.

Tillich, Paul. "You Are Accepted." In *The Shaking of the Foundations.* New York: Charles Scribner's Sons, 1948.

Underhill, Evelyn. *Worship.* New York: Oxford University Press, 1967.

Vidich, Arthur, and Bensman, Joseph. *Small Town in Mass Society.* Princeton: Princeton University Press, 1958.

Westerhoff, John H.III. *Will Our Children Have Faith?* New York: Seabury Press, 1976.

White, James F. *New Forms of Worship.* Nashville: Abingdon Press, 1971.

————. *The Worldliness of Worship.* New York: Oxford University Press, 1967.

White, Phyllis C. *The Broadly Graded Group: A Manual for Children in the Church.* Memphis: Board of Christian Education, Cumberland Presbyterian Church, 1981.

Willimon, William H. *Word, Water, Wine and Bread.* Valley Forge, PA: Judson Press, 1980.

Willimon, William H., and Wilson, Robert L. *Preaching and Worship in the Small Church.* Nashville: Abingdon Press, 1980.

Winter, Miriam Therese. *Preparing the Way of the Lord.* Nashville: Abingdon Press, 1978.

Wolff, Kurt H. *The Sociology of Georg Simmel.* New York: Free Press, 1950.

Periodicals and Reports

Brown, David J.; Haskins, Robert; and Swisher, William. "Small Church Project." United Church Board for Homeland Ministries. New York, 1977.

Christian Ministry, July 1977.

Dailey, Charles A. "The Management of Conflict." *The Chicago Theological Seminary Register,* May 1969, p. 7.

Dudley, Carl S. "Small Churches Are Special." *JED Share,* Spring 1979, pp. 4-5.

———. "The Unique Dynamics of the Small Church." Alban Institute, Washington, DC, 1977.

Good to Be Together. UCC Office for Church Life and Leadership, 1976.

Grassroots 2, Winter 1978, The Resource Center for Small Churches, Luling, TX.

Hutcheson, Richard G. Jr. "Pluralism and Consensus: Why Mainline Church Mission Budgets Are in Trouble," *The Christian Century,* 6-13 July 1977, pp. 619-21.

Lowery, James. L. Jr. "The Small Church Is Here to Stay and She Can Be Viable." Enablement, Inc., Boston, 1974.